Society for Promoting the Abolition of Slavery

Centennial Anniversary of the Pennsylvania Society

For Promoting the Abolition of Slavery, the Relief of Free Negroes...

Society for Promoting the Abolition of Slavery

Centennial Anniversary of the Pennsylvania Society
For Promoting the Abolition of Slavery, the Relief of Free Negroes...

ISBN/EAN: 9783744735087

Printed in Europe, USA, Canada, Australia, Japan

Cover: Foto ©ninafisch / pixelio.de

More available books at **www.hansebooks.com**

CENTENNIAL ANNIVERSARY

OF THE

Pennsylvania Society,

FOR

PROMOTING THE ABOLITION OF SLAVERY,

THE

RELIEF OF FREE NEGROES UNLAWFULLY HELD IN BONDAGE; AND
FOR IMPROVING THE CONDITION OF THE AFRICAN RACE.

PHILADELPHIA:
GRANT, FAIRES & RODGERS, PRINTERS.
1876.

CENTENNIAL ANNIVERSARY

OF THE

Pennsylvania Society,

FOR

PROMOTING THE ABOLITION OF SLAVERY,

THE

RELIEF OF FREE NEGROES UNLAWFULLY HELD IN BONDAGE: AND FOR
IMPROVING THE CONDITION OF THE AFRICAN RACE.

PHILADELPHIA:
GRANT, FAIRES & RODGERS, PRINTERS.
1875.

OFFICERS FOR 1875.

— —

PRESIDENT.
DILLWYN PARRISH.

VICE PRESIDENTS.
BENJAMIN COATES,   T. ELLWOOD CHAPMAN.

SECRETARIES.
JOSEPH M. TRUMAN, JR.,   WILLIAM HEACOCK.

TREASURER.
CALEB CLOTHIER.

LIBRARIAN.
JOSEPH M. TRUMAN, JR.

RECORDER OF MANUMISSIONS.
CALEB CLOTHIER.

COUNSELLORS.
EDWARD HOPPER, Philadelphia.
GEORGE H. EARLE,   "
JOSEPH R. RHOADS,   "
D. NEWLIN FELL,   "
JOSEPH J. LEWIS, Chester.

ACTING COMMITTEE.
DILLWYN PARRISH,   PASSMORE WILLIAMSON,
WM. J. MULLEN,   ALFRED H. LOVE,
HENRY M. LAING,   O. HOWARD WILSON,
WILLIAM STILL.

BOARD OF EDUCATION.
BENJAMIN COATES,   T. ELLWOOD CHAPMAN,
DILLWYN PARRISH,   BENJAMIN P. HUNT,
WM. HEACOCK,   JOS. M. TRUMAN, JR.,
WILLIAM STILL,   MORDECAI BUZBY,
HENRY M. LAING,   MARCELLUS BALDERSTON,
O. HOWARD WILSON,   WILLIAM WHIPPER,
LUKENS WEBSTER.

COMMITTEE ON PROPERTY.
CALEB CLOTHIER,   WILLIAM J. MULLEN,
T. ELLWOOD CHAPMAN.

CENTENNIAL ANNIVERSARY.

The "Pennsylvania Society for Promoting the Abolition of Slavery, the Relief of Free Negroes Unlawfully Held in Bondage, and for Improving the Condition of the African Race," celebrated its Centennial Anniversary at Concert Hall, in Philadelphia, Wednesday, April 14th, 1875. The organization is the oldest and most efficient of all that rallied around the same humane cause, but has received less recognition than others that accomplished no tithe of its work.

The history of the Society touches that of the Western Continent. Spain enslaved and exported Indians here as early as 1495. The difficulty of procuring Indians and the need for labor induced the Spaniards to import negroes to the New World soon after. The Emperor Charles V. licensed a Fleming to ship negroes to the West Indies. Other European nations imitated this conduct, and slavery was naturalized. Before 1776 more than 300,000 negroes arrived. The Continental Congress forbade the importation to the United States in 1776, but Congress was forbidden by the Constitution to stop the trade before 1808, although Washington, Hamilton, Jefferson, Jay, Franklin, Madison and many of their great cotemporaries saw its conflict with the Declaration and opposed its tolerance. They hoped, however, that an institution so foreign to the genius of the land, to Christianity, education, civilization and industry would die from its own baseness, and shrank from awakening sectional feeling and interfering with business interests. They even conceded to the South some advantages for preserving the system, under a conviction that it must die there as it had died at the North. The politicians and merchants were foremost in this compromise between right and wrong, and the mass of the people were not unwilling abettors. The old Abolition Society did not participate in this dangerous and costly blunder. They were sagacious, principled and humane men. Revolting from an inhumanity so

3

gross, inexcusable and dangerous, they associated to effect by concert what they dared not attempt individually : proclaimed their intent and undertook what none lived to see realized.

One of the first important steps of the Society was the last important public act of Benjamin Franklin. He as President signed a Memorial addressed by the Society to Congress in 1790, asking that body " to devise means for removing the inconsistency of slavery from the American people," and " to step to the very verge of its power for discouraging every species of traffic in the persons of our fellow-men." The history of the doings of this old Abolition Society is unwritten; and they are so involved in all that was attempted and done by either political party to render the land free in fact as in name, and in all the vexed questions of a century, that they can hardly ever be dissociated. But the individuals who adhered to the truth, and defended the common cause of government, of constitutional law, of human rights and national well-being in hopeless days, and by this devotion bred the sense that finally won their wishes—these individuals will be loved for their truth and honored for their conduct always. They were crushed, and even hope itself seemed lost when the Fugitive Slave Law enacted more than ever had been conceded, and carried the slave-master under the escort of civil power, with a right to demand military assistance, into every free State. Still they believed that Right lived " the eternal years of God," and were undismayed by the momentary defeat and stimulated to greater effort. Despite growing obloquy not unattended by personal danger and loss of property, they retained their faith and continued their labors ; they ameliorated the condition of some and succored the wants of others, enslaved or fugitive ; reunited families that had escaped and placed them in safety ; and when the old members were gathered to the majority, full of years and full of honors, confident of their reward, their children filled their places as worthily and enlisted others,—among them those who now exult in the fruition of a hope so long delayed—the attainment of a purpose so necessary for the nation and human progress.

The first object of the Society has been realized. On all the continent no slave now draws breath ; and those who remain enslaved on its adjacent islands can foresee the date of their final emancipation. The Society is now remitted to its second purpose—the improvement of the condition of the African race ; a labor as great perhaps as its predecessor,—certainly as important to the nation, the race and the world ; and that is to be prosecuted steadily, against many discouragements as well as under many encouragements, until the whole end of the early organization has been fulfilled in every detail and to the spirit as well as to the letter.

The following is the Programme of Exercises, as issued by the Committee.

1775. CENTENNIAL ANNIVERSARY 1875.

OF THE

PENNSYLVANIA SOCIETY

FOR PROMOTING THE ABOLITION OF SLAVERY,

TO BE HELD AT CONCERT HALL,

CHESTNUT ST., ABOVE TWELFTH,

On Wednesday Afternoon, April 14th, 1875,

AT 2½ O'CLOCK, P. M.

SINGING BY THE HUTCHINSON FAMILY.

PROGRAMME.

CHAIRMAN:

HON. HENRY WILSON, *Vice President of United States.*

PRAYER,	REV. W. H. FURNESS, D. D.
HISTORICAL ORATION,	DR. WM. ELDER.

ADDRESSES BY

FREDERICK DOUGLASS,	LUCRETIA MOTT,	ELIZUR WRIGHT, JR.,
ROBERT PURVIS,	MRS. F. E. W. HARPER,	C. C. BURLEIGH,
HON. W. S. PEIRCE,	BISHOP D. A. PAYNE,	Prof. J. M. LANGSTON,
A. M. POWELL,	ABBY KELLEY FORSTER,	and others.

DOXOLOGY.

BENEDICTION,

BISHOP CAMPBELL.

☞ The above Speakers will participate in the Evening Exercises, to be held at Bethel Church, Sixth below Pine, at 7½ o'clock, P. M.

COMMITTEE OF ARRANGEMENTS.

WM. STILL,	DILLWYN PARRISH,	JOSEPH M. TRUMAN, JR.,
Chairman,	PASSMORE WILLIAMSON,	HENRY M. LAING.

700 Arch Street.

At the appointed hour, Wednesday afternoon, April 14th, William Still, Chairman of the Committee of Arrangements, called the meeting to order. The stand was properly decorated with the national ensign, and bouquets of tasteful flowers adorned the desk. Conspicuous on either side of the Chairman, were men eminent in the annals of the Society and in the affairs of the Union. Hon. Henry Wilson, Vice-President of the United States, occupied the central seat in the front row. Frederick Douglass, the eminent and eloquent champion of his race sat near; supported by the gifted orator, Robert Purvis, and countenanced by Lucretia Mott, Abby Kelley Foster, and others scarcely less known. Members of the Society of Friends were conspicuous everywhere, and tempered the brilliant colors of the assembly by the sedate tone of their attire. They who had done so much to make the Centennial possible were very properly prominent in its observance. Ex-Governor Curtin, C. C. Burleigh, Prof. Langston, Bishop Campbell, Passmore Williamson, Elizur Wright, Henry Armitt Brown, Esq., Dillwyn Parrish, Frances E. W. Harper, Hon. W. S. Peirce, H. M. Laing, Sarah Pugh, Simon Barnard, Cyrus Elder, Rachel W. Townsend, Geo. Alsop, Yardley Warner, Hannah Cox, Dinah Mendenhall, Geo.W. Taylor, Elijah F. Pennypacker, and others whose services won the honor, were grouped on the stage, in the sight of a large audience. The President of the Society then called the assemblage to order, and announced that the Hon. Henry Wilson, Vice-President of the United States, would preside. He, coming forward, acknowledged the reception accorded him and called upon Rev. W. H. Furness, D. D., to invoke the Divine blessing upon the meeting. Dr. Furness did so as follows:

THE INVOCATION.

Oh Thou, Ever-Present and All-surrounding Maker and Lord of all things, Thou hast Thy being in us as we have our being in Thee. We invoke now the inspiration and the blessing of Thy felt presence in our hearts. We rejoice that while there are so many occasions of strife and of separation among men, there is yet one cause for which strangers may meet as friends, as brothers and sisters of one household. Thus coming together now, we rejoice in the manifestation of Thy Spirit, in the precious memories which this day brings upon the cause of freedom and humanity, ever advancing even from the smallest beginnings to the great triumph which it has been our privilege to witness. Thou hast given us to see what wise and faithful men, martyrs, and prophets longed to see, but never saw save in prophetic vision. Truly is Thy doing marvellous in our eyes. Not unto us, not unto men be the glory; for no flesh can glory in Thy most manifest presence.

And now with one heart do we pray that the heart of this great nation may not die and lie buried under the mountain of its worldly prosperity; but may our just and equal institutions have their due influence, and day by day and hour by hour may they breathe into the hearts of this people that sacred sentiment of human respect which must be the life of our life, and which shall so expand all hearts that the fetters of pride and prejudice shall fall away, even as the chains have fallen from the limbs of the slave. May Thy kingdom come, O God! the kingdom of Thy truth and justice, and Thy will be done on earth as it is done by the angels of Thy presence. Give us this day and at this hour what is needful for our souls; may we forgive as we hope to be forgiven. Lead us not into temptation, but deliver us from evil: for Thine is the kingdom, the power and the glory, forever and ever.

ADDRESS BY THE VICE-PRESIDENT OF THE UNITED STATES.

Hon. Henry Wilson, Vice-President of the United States, then delivered a Commemorative oration, with an earnest eloquence attested by his long sympathy for and aid of the Society, that was inspired by patriotic joy and national pride, and riveted the unflagging attention of the great audience, who drowned its conclusion in applause. The Oration was as follows:

LADIES AND GENTLEMEN: The duty of presiding over the proceedings of this day has been assigned me by the Board of Managers. Gratefully I accept this position, and at once enter upon the performance of its duties. To be chosen to preside over this centennial celebration of the anniversary of a society established for purposes such as those for which this society was established, and actuated by motives such as those which actuated this society—enrolling among its members names so illustrious, and accomplishing a work so grand—is to me one of the happiest and proudest events of my life. [Applause.] The organization of this society a century ago was indeed a great event, and its history is one of the purest, grandest, and noblest of any organization in the history of the world. Its effect and influence in the early days of the Republic were seen and acknowledged. Its labors at a later period—at the time when the cruel fugitive slave act was being executed in the country—were seen and felt;

and the evidences of those labors were manifested in this city, in the counties around about you, and in the border counties of Pennsylvania. The country has never known more faithful men—and women, too—than have been connected with the Pennsylvania Abolition Society. There is to-day, thank God, no slave in the Republic! [Applause.] The fetters were not melted off by kindly influences, but were stricken off by the rude hand of civil war. The chains fell not from the limbs of the slave by the conversion of the master, but by the interposition of the strong hand of power. And, ladies and gentlemen, remember to-day, on this hundredth anniversary of the organization of this great society, that the work for which this society was organized is not yet accomplished. The slave is free, but the system of slavery left behind it influences, and powers, and scars which only the humanity, the Christianity of the American people can work away. Dr. Furness alluded to the falling of the chains from the limbs of the slave, and has prayed to God that the time might come when human passions and prejudices might so fall away. The thought is a beautiful one. Humane Christianity! It should be the vital, animating spirit of this nation to work away these prejudices, to lift up the poor and the lowly, and make the Republic that which in deed and in truth it ought to be—a Christian land, where every man is fully protected in his rights as a citizen.

I fear, ladies and gentlemen, that there is in the country to-day, a counter-revolution against the colored man. It must be met by the men whose hearts are bathed in the anti-slavery sentiment, and who mean, God blessing us, that the spirit of anti-slavery shall pervade the whole land, North and South. [Applause.] Let it be understood, then, henceforth and forever, that no matter what time it takes, no matter what it costs, the sentiment of the Abolition Society of Pennsylvania, with that of kindred and more recent organizations, must pervade this land; that the condition of the colored men must be improved; that the condition of the poor white men who suffered by slavery must be improved—aye, too, that the condition of that deluded but smitten and stricken section of our country must be improved. Let it be understood then that while we love the black man, and mean to lift him up, to elevate and protect him, and to aid him in the grand work of self-improvement, we also mean to lift up, elevate, and improve the poor-white men whom slavery smote. Aye, and we mean to improve the condition of the erring and sinning masses, and to build up our country and make our country what it ought to be—an example and an inspiration for the nations. [Great applause.] ·

The Hutchinson Family sang one of the melodies they made familiar in former years.

Robert Purvis, Esq., was introduced to read the letters of invited guests who were unable to attend. He said as a preliminary:

Mr. Chairman: Of the letters that are placed in my hands I shall read but a few. The first is from the great Pioneer; the man who caught the inspiration from the pamphlet of the Quaker girl in England, who, as against gradualism, declared the doctrine of immediatism as alike the right of the slave and the duty of the master. This letter, sir, is from William Lloyd Garrison. [Applause.] It reads as follows:

Boston, April 12, 1875.

Dear Mr. Still: Honored with a pressing invitation to participate in the Centennial anniversary of the Pennsylvania Society for the Promotion of the Abolition of Slavery, etc., to be celebrated in Philadelphia on the 14th instant, I can only return my thanks for the same, regretting that circumstances oblige me to be absent. This celebration is certainly as suggestive as it is unique. An Anti-slavery Society a century old! And of that long period only the last ten years have witnessed the abolition of that inhuman slave system, in opposition to which the Society was organized! Half a million of slaves at the commencement multiplying to four millions before their emancipation! Ninety years of persistent, active, shameless slave-holding, slave-hunting, slave-trading, by a people claiming to have Christ for their divine examplar, the Bible for their only rule of faith and practice, and genuine democracy as the pole-star of their political form of government! Ninety years of sinful compromises to perpetuate an oppression, "one hour of which," so testified Thomas Jefferson, "was fraught with more misery than ages of that which our fathers rose in rebellion to oppose!" Ninety years busily occupied in an insane attempt to bring into concord light and darkness, God and Mammon, Christ and Belial, and to make homogeneous ideas, customs, and institutions inherently antagonistical! And this awful state of things at last ending, not in a general repentance and contrition, but by a bloody retribution long ago predicted, and for many years admonishingly set forth by the true friends of equal rights, if justice were not speedily done. "Thus saith the Lord: Ye have not hearkened unto me, in proclaiming liberty, every one to his brother, and every man to his neighbor: behold, I proclaim a, liberty for you, saith the Lord, to the sword, to the pestilence, and to the famine." What a record of hypocrisy and double-dealing!

Will it be said that the past, with whatever of shame or guilt attaches to it, ought to be buried in oblivion ; that, as not a slave is left to clank his fetters in all the land, conciliation and good-will are the duties of the hour; that to revive such recollections can only tend to perpetuate feelings of alienation and bitterness? Suggestions like these have a plausible sound, but they are illusory. Our progress in unity, in all that tends to make a people truly great and prosperous, will be exactly in proportion to our willingness to contemplate the causes of our fearful visitations, that we may all the more earnestly "study the things that make for peace," by securing to all the inhabitants of the land their God-given rights, so that neither under the National nor any State government shall there be any intolerance toward any class on the American soil. Admitting that we have many reasons for "thanking God and taking courage," I think that there are also many others which should serve to stimulate us to earnest and persistent action in well-doing by remembering that " the price of liberty is eternal vigilance." May your celebration be in all respects worthy of the event!

Yours, for universal freedom,   Wm. Lloyd Garrison.

Letters regretting the inability of the writers to be present were also received from Wendell Phillips of Massachusetts, John G. Whittier of Massachusetts, President U. S. Grant, George W. Curtis of New York, John Needles of Maryland, Rev. John Sargeant of Massachusetts, Joseph A. Dugdale of Iowa, Rev. Samuel May of Boston, Rev. R. Collyer of Illinois, James G. Thompson of South Carolina, George W. Julian of Indiana, Edmund Quincy of Massachusetts, Gen. B. F. Butler of Massachusetts, Gov. Hartranft, Mayor Stokley and A. B. Bradford of Pennsylvania, R. F. Walcott of Massachusetts, A. M. Powell of Massachusetts, Samuel M. Janney of Virginia, Rev. C. B. Ray of New York, Rev. John F. Sargeant of Massachusetts, Rev. George Whipple of New York, John P. Green of Ohio, and Rev. O. B. Frothingham of New York, and Geo. F. McFarland. Brief extracts from these were read.

Amesbury, 24th Third Month, 1875.

Dillwyn Parrish:—My dear Friend:—I regret more than I can express that I cannot be with thee and other dear old friends and co-workers in the cause of freedom on the occasion of the Centennial Anniversary of the Pennsylvania Abolition Society.

For, indeed, it is an event of no ordinary significance, this centennial of the first society ever formed for the abolition of slavery.

It commemorates one of the great aggressive movements of Christian civilization against the still surviving barbarism of an age of brute force and selfishness.

ii

What a history is connected with it! What a struggle between all that is best and all that is vilest in human nature has marked its progress! What faith, what courage, what noble aspirations, what generous self-sacrifice has it known! How many blessings from souls rescued from the intolerable hell of slavery have made the sleep of its members sweeter and compensated them for their life-long labors! Looking over its roll of membership, we find the names of men whose memory is precious—the elect and called of God to the noblest service—men every way worthy of a State whose foundations were laid in prayer, and to whose charter of rights and liberties the joint wisdom of Penn and Sydney contributed.

The great Centennial of American Independence of the coming year will show that no State has a prouder record than Pennsylvania: but in all her rich inheritance of renown she has nothing better than her Abolition Society, the first of its kind in the world's history, numbering among its supporters such men as Franklin, Baldwin, Rush, Pemberton, Mifflin, Shipley, Needles, and thy own honored father.

The world slowly emerging from the darkness of the Stone Age, still, doubtless, over-estimates its warrior champions; but the time is not far distant when justice will be done to the heroes of the bloodless victories of Christian civilization and progress.

> Their armor rings on a fairer field
> Than Greek or Trojan ever trod;
> For freedom's sword is the blade they wield,
> And the light above is the smile of God.

So far as the abolition of slavery is concerned, the work of the society is done. Mainly upon the colored people themselves now depends the question whether, by patient industry, sobriety and assiduous self-culture, they shall overcome the unchristian prejudice still existing against them, or by indolence, thriftlessness, and moral and physical degradation, they shall confirm and strengthen it.

But there is on the part of all who have sought their freedom, no lack of occasion for labor in their behalf in accordance with the very spirit and letter of the constitution of the Pennsylvania Abolition Society, which is pledged to "the relief of free negroes."

All that can be done consistent with the constitutional right of States, should be done for their protection by the General Government, and there is no philanthropic object at the present time more deserving of encouragement than that of the education of the children of freedmen.

In this point of view there is still work for the old parent society, and it has a legitimate right to exist and continue its labors of love so long as there is prejudice to overcome or ignorance to be enlightened.

Accept, dear friend, assurances of old-time love and respect from thy friend. JOHN G. WHITTIER.

THE HISTORICAL ORATION.

DR. WILLIAM ELDER was then introduced by the chairman with some complimentary remarks, observing that he needed no introduction to a Pennsylvania audience. Dr. Elder spoke extemporaneously, and discussed the progress of Abolition from the first suggestion to its victory, as follows:

LADIES AND GENTLEMEN: In assuming to discharge the duty which has been requested and required of me by the Committee of Arrangements, I shall follow the line of thought which has been designated for me by the committee. It is unfortunate that in this instance they should have selected "the wrong man" for "the right place;" inasmuch as the subject of which I am to treat being of an historical character, and therefore necessarily dependent mainly upon facts and dates, should properly be presented from written notes, whereas my habit has been during all my life to speak extemporaneously. I once tried to read in public a lecture, but it was the only time I ever essayed such a task. Aside from that, there is this consideration: the facts and the dates that go to make up the history of this hundred years whose close you are now here to celebrate, and the circumstances and influences that hover around that momentous era, cannot now be memorized—nay, it is impossible to read them to you because they have as yet not all been written, and the day has not yet come when they can be fully comprehended. If stated with only comparative accuracy and amplitude, what a compendium of events, what a chronology would not that history comprise—what a host of memories would rise up to confront us here to-day! Who now can faithfully trace the current and river of this great anti-slavery influence to the rills and brooks and spring-tops and mountain-heads from which it started? I repeat, I do not think the time has yet come when even the best of us can fully comprehend this influence. I know not in which direction the most powerful springs of action are to be traced. Sometimes I have thought it was to the leading minds of the times, and that history would so record it. Again, it has occurred to me that in my own experience it was in the common heart of the masses of the people that I had found the strongest resources for the little labor that I may have performed in the cause. The epoch in which your Society had its origin is marked by events such as these. In 1776, Friends' Yearly Meeting took the decisive step of subjecting to discipline and disownment members who held slaves over lawful age. Emancipations about this time became very frequent, both within and without the Quaker community. Without following any exact order in point of date, the facts are that in 1778 Jefferson had a bill passed by the Legislature of Virginia abolishing the foreign slave trade—I mean prohibiting the importation of slaves into that State. In 1787 he provided, in the bill for the cession to the old Confederacy of the Northwestern Territory, (embracing within it the territorial limits of the States of Ohio, Indiana, and Illinois), that slavery should cease forever in that large domain after the year 1800; this provision, which was introduced by the Virginia Legislature, being identical in terms with that of the celebrated Wilmot Proviso offered in 1846 in respect to any and all territory that should be acquired from Mexico. In 1772 the famous Somerset case was decided by Lord Mansfield, though Chief Justice Holeton's decision was made in much stronger terms at least eighty years before. The Chief Justice decided that no law of England ever made a slave; that "there were villeins indeed, but no chattel slaves;" that the absolute right to the body of a man was not English. Jefferson's Notes on the State of Virginia, printed in Paris in 1784, contained the famous passage, with which you are all familiar: "The Almighty has no attribute that could take part with us in a servile war; I tremble for my country when I feel that God is just."

In 1780 the Legislature of Pennsylvania passed the act for the gradual abolition of slavery in this State. In 1770, Granville Sharpe first appears in the conduct of the Somerset case. Clarkson and Wilberforce must be dated about the year 1785, and William Pitt, chief of the Ministry, and Charles James Fox, leader of the Opposition, joined in antagonism to the slave trade in 1790. The English House of Commons passed a bill for the suppression of the slave trade in 1793 and again in 1794, which bill failed in the House of Peers, but was finally passed in 1807. In 1777 the State of Vermont passed an act abolishing slavery in that State. At that time Vermont had less than three hundred slaves within her territory. Pennsylvania, when she abolished her system of slavery, held nearly four thousand slaves. According to the interpretation of her constitution subsequently rendered by the Supreme Court, Massachusetts abolished slavery in 1780 by her constitution. On the 15th of May, 1791, France, by her National Assembly, virtually granted equal political rights to free men, without regard to color.

To this list I now add the date of the organization of your own Society. It was organized on the 14th of April, 1775, with John Baldwin as its President, and Thomas Harrison as its Secretary; with whom were very soon associated, in sentiment and in action, men whose names are leading and inextinguishable in the history of our country. In 1787 Benjamin Franklin was elected President and Dr. Benjamin Rush one of its Secretaries. The list embraces some two hundred and forty-four names.

These facts and dates define and embrace the time of the National birthday of the United States of America, and the whole period is marked by an epidemic of abolitionism, both in these States and the whole of Western Europe.

Here I am led to remark that while a history looks up the day-springs of the great events which it narrates, there is not in reality, either in science, morals, or politics, any means of fixing the dates of discoveries so absolutely as to mark with precision the areas of their great revolutions. These dates are in facts as inconclusive as was Topsy's genealogy, who, when asked who made her, replied, "I dunno : I 'spect I growed." The greatest and gravest of the received authorities seems compelled to declare that it was *in the beginning* that God made the heavens and the earth, and no more definite date can be given to any great event which He has inspired. Exactly where one wave of the ocean begins or ends is not seen ; it is only toward their crests that they become clearly distinct. We must, therefore, content ourselves with stating in general that in this wickedness of personal slavery the whole world lay until some time about the middle of the eighteenth century, when a new world of men and things began to emerge, so fruitful of wonders during its first century of progress that no tongue can tell, no mind can comprehend them. About this epoch the spirit of reform moved abroad on the face of the earth, and the greater and lesser lights gathered into suns, and moons, and stars, and divided the day from the night; moral, religious, and political liberty broke into insurrection and revolution, and their course has ever since run from victory to victory, "leading captivity captive," until now, upon the great centennial of our own national history, the chattel slavery of man in the whole civilized world is dead. Who is sufficient for these things? What colossal intellect can retrace even the topmost stepping-stones that marked the progress of the last half of the eighteenth century in the abolishment of the slaveries of every form which hung upon it at its beginning ? Think of the biographical dictionary that should hold the deeds of the heroes of this great history. Think of the chronological list that would give their dates. We turn now to a second period of our history. A member of the convention which formed our Federal Constitution, upon returning to his Massachusetts constituency, felicitated them with the announcement that they had given slavery its death-blow. Yet that was twenty years before Congress abolished the foreign slave trade of the United States. Even then the atmosphere of the whole civilized world was bright in the light of anti-slavery sentiment and abolition effort. At this time (the period of the formation of the Federal Constitution), Franklin and Rush presided over the labors of the Pennsylvania Society: John Jay and Alexander Hamilton were President and Vice-president of the New York Manumission Society. Other associations were formed in the other Eastern States, and they were vigorous and hopeful in the South; in Virginia, Delaware, Maryland, Kentucky, Georgia, and North Carolina. The doctrines of these associations went, I think, no further than gradual abolition. What Franklin and his associates meant by asking Congress, in 1790, to " devise means for removing the inconsistency of slavery from the American people, and to step to the very verge of its power for discouraging every species of traffic in the persons of our fellow-men," is easily inferred. This petition, signed by Franklin as the president of your Society, was sent to the first Congress, at not later than its second session.

Now the third epoch of this eventful history opens upon us. After the achievements and triumphs of the times of 1776 and the abolition of the foreign slave trade of the United States, there was a lull in the movement of the people of these two countries until, in 1819, the Missouri question awakened the slumbering energies of the Northern States. During the period of this comparative inaction the phase in the fortunes of our colored people had been steadily assuming portentous features. In 1793 Whitney produced his cotton gin for the separation of the seed from the fibre. Before that a negro woman could not clean more than one pound in a day. Whitney's machine finished three hundred weight per diem, or did three hundred and thirty times the amount of work that a slave could perform. This made the cotton production very profitable, and slavery, employed in the culture of the plant, rose proportionately in value. Somewhere between 1807 and 1820 the invention of machinery and the application of steam in the manufacture into all the forms of use brought into the field of this warfare an auxiliary to the slavery forces that, for a long while, was perfectly irresistible. Humanity, morality, political consistency, national honor, and national safety—all were overpowered, and the extension of slavery to new territory and the acquisition of other new territory for its extension became the ruling policy of the South and of their sympathizers in the North.

In this state of things the first square fight between the parties came upon us in 1819–20. The old love of liberty aroused, struggled manfully and bravely, but the axe had not been laid at the root of the tree in the Revolutionary period; only some of its branches had been lopped off, while others grew into great strength under the fostering influence of the golden showers that Trade poured upon them. The contest of that day was lost to the friends of Liberty. In the trial hour, when the result of the battle hung upon a doubt, the Great Compromiser came into the struggle, won his title of Pacificator, and for long years afterwards the compromisers, pacificators, and Union-savers left behind them the strife they had so often settled and compromised, to be finally settled and pacificated by the bayonet.

After the defeat of 1818–20 the losing party began to look to the efficiency of the weapons they had used in the battle which they had so sadly lost. They saw that in this Republic Cotton had become King de facto, and that slavery had absolutely reached the sovereignty. They could not submit to defeat, though the glaring fact confronted them that slaves of not more than the average market price of $25 in 1790 had risen to $300 before 1830, while their number had swollen from not quite seven hundred thousand to above three millions. Gradual abolition and assistance to negroes unlawfully held in bondage had utterly failed of their hopes.

These weapons struck wide of the mark. The system of slavery itself was clearly the heart and source of all the evils engendered by it, and they now knew that at that vital point every blow must be aimed. Granville Sharpe, as early as 1787, in a society formed in London, for the suppression of the slave trade, insisted upon opposing slavery also. In this he was, perhaps, twenty years ahead of his compeers, Wilberforce and Clarkson. The next earliest I have met with was Elizabeth Heyrick, of London, I believe, who, in 1823, published a pamphlet entitled "Immediate, Not Gradual, Emancipation." The friends of the great cause, however, did not immediately adopt the doctrine; they graduated slowly through gradualism, or colonization, until they finally took the vantage ground of Immediateism. And there they stood, without dodging or apology, through terrible trials and sufferings, until the common foe awoke the common wrath of the whole nation, and Abraham Lincoln officially gave the foe the *coup de grace* which Granville Sharpe and Elizabeth Heyrick meant for it. The armies of the Union empowered him to deal " the stroke of mercy," that at once put the monster out of the field of battle, and out of his pain in dying.

The next Immediatist who stands conspicuously in the story of this struggle is Benjamin Lundy, who, beginning in 1815 in St. Clairsville, Ohio, there organized a society of five hundred members. Soon afterwards he purchased out of his scanty means a newspaper, and devoted it entirely to the promotion of the anti-slavery cause. He removed this paper, which he called *The Genius of Universal Emancipation*, to Baltimore; where, in 1829, Wm. Lloyd Garrison joined him in its editorial management. Lundy connected colonization with his scheme, favoring Texas or Hayti, or other suitable localities, as the promised land for the great modern exodus from our Egypt. He has never, perhaps, been exceeded in zeal, labor, and sacrifice by any philanthropist. Mr. Garrison himself was a distinguished Colonizationist, and in Baltimore, in 1830, he was imprisoned for alleged libel published upon a slave-trader, and for disturbing the public peace. His trials and labors then began. I cannot detail them if I would. I need not if I could.

About 1840-41, the date of the establishment of *The Liberator*, the strife began that was destined to introduce the fifth and last act of this grand tragedy. This fourth period, covering the thirty years' war of arguments for weapons; a war under the forms of peace; a war at once defensive and aggressive was a battle to the death, yet a battle that "took from conquest its crime, and from victory its chains." On one side was arrayed the slave*owner* of the South, and the slave*holder* of the North; on the other, the many-headed mass of the friends of Liberty. Slavery now no longer stood the apologist of its attendant evils, but the bold prosecutor of the disturbers of the public peace. Everything that malice and fear could suggest, the monster practiced. It bribed and bullied our politicians; it dominated the press; it profaned the pulpit; it put its livery upon religion, and dressed our philosophy in its cap and bells; it denied the right of petition to our people; it branded our birthright, liberty of speech, as incendiary; it proposed to censure one of our representatives for asking whether a petition from slaves might be offered in the Federal House of Representatives, and well-nigh killed one of our senators in his seat because of his steady and persistent defence of public justice. It repealed all that had any good in it of the Missouri Compromise; it inaugurated a war with Mexico for the extension of its territorial dominion, and "snaked in" Texas, with a territory six times the size of Massachu-

2

setts, and doomed it to slavery. This move in regard to Texas it accomplished under the forms of an international treaty, when it could not have accomplished it under any form of law or precedent. And it finally decided that the colored people had "no rights which white men were bound to respect."

At the close of the rebellion we had upon our hands, say, four millions of slaves. Immediateism then boldly undertook the risks and performed the duty of emancipating this host—a host greater by far in number than was that which Moses was able to conduct in safety through the desert into the promised land. What are the results?

England emancipated her slaves mainly because they were worthless as property to their masters, but urged, also doubtless by sentiments of religion and morality; but 70,000 of her emancipated countrymen were hung in the reign of Henry VIII. Now, in relative ratio to population, this number of executions for crime would equal, in the population of Pennsylvania, five victims per day. These homeless wretches were hung for burglary, larceny, trespass, and vagrancy—for all the offences that poverty and destitution could suggest. This experience strengthened the argument against emancipation in this country. But behold! Our freedmen have passed into citizenship in the face of prejudice and of every burden that they could be made to bear, without arsons, murders, riots, or such impoverishment as seemed clearly impending upon them. The purity of the principle and the righteousness of the policy are vindicated now and forever by the fact that these people have passed from bondage into freedom more safely than have any other people in the world's wide history.

The Hutchinson Family sang Whittier's "Furnace Blast," at the close of Dr. Elder's oration, in such a manner and with such spirit that it elicited great applause.

THE FURNACE BLAST.

We wait beneath the furnace-blast
The pangs of transformation;
Not painlessly doth God recast
And mould anew the nation.
    Hot burns the fire
    Where wrongs expire;
    Nor spares the hand
    That from the land
Uproots the ancient evil.

The hand-breadth cloud the sages feared
Its bloody rain is dropping;

The poison plant the fathers spared
All else is overtopping.
  East, West, South, North,
  It curses the earth ;
  All justice dies,
  And fraud and lies
Live only in its shadow.

What gives the wheat-field blades of steel?
  What points the rebel cannon ?
What sets the roaring rabble's heel
  On the old star-spangled pennon ?
    What breaks the oath
    Of the men o' the South
    For the Union's life ?—
  Hark to the answer: Slavery !

Then waste no blows on lesser foes
  In strife unworthy freemen.
God lifts to-day the vail, and shows
  The features of the demon !
    O North and South,
    Its victims both,
    Can ye not cry,
    " Let slavery die !"
  And union find in freedom ?

What though the cast-out spirit tear
  The nation in his going ?
We who have shared the guilt must share
  The pang of his o'erthrowing !
    Whate'er the loss,
    Whate'er the cross,
    Shall they complain
    Of present pain
  Who trust in God's hereafter?

For who that leans on His right arm
  Was ever yet forsaken ?
What righteous cause can suffer harm
  If He its part has taken ?
    Though wild and loud
    And dark the cloud
    Behind its folds
    His hand upholds
  The calm sky of to-morrow !

Above the maddening cry for blood,
Above the wild war-drumming,
Let Freedom's voice be heard, with good
The evil overcoming.
Give prayer and purse
To stay the Curse
Whose wrong we share,
Whose shame we bear,
Whose end shall gladden Heaven !

In vain the bells of war shall ring
Of triumphs and revenges,
While still is spared the evil thing
That severs and estranges.
But blest the ear
That yet shall hear
The jubilant bell
That rings the knell
Of Slavery forever !

Then let the selfish lip be dumb,
And hushed the breath of sighing ;
Before the joy of peace must come
The pains of purifying.
God give us grace
Each in his place
To bear his lot,
And, murmuring not,
Endure, and wait, and labor !

The president then addressed the audience and said :

LADIES AND GENTLEMEN : The words of the Quaker poet, Whittier, to
which you have just listened, could not be sung in the early winter of
1861 in the army of the Potomac without causing military interference.
I thank God those words can be sung to-day on every square mile of the
Republic. [Applause.]

I now have the honor of presenting to you a gentleman born in the
State of Maryland, a victim of the slave system, who struck that system
heavy blows, and who has won a name in the cause of liberty that history
will record. I present to you Frederick Douglass. [Long-continued
applause.]

This fine compliment to the veteran orator of the colored race met a
hearty response from the large assemblage. The speaker's comparison of
the centennial anniversary which they were celebrating and the one to

come off next year in this city—as he showed that while the Exposition
in 1876 is to celebrate nationality, this is to celebrate universal humanity: his allusion to the distinguished men and women who had reached out
a friendly hand to the negroes when they escaped from slavery, and his
declaration of the negro's wants—protection to his rights and education ;
his powerful description of the condition of the negro to-day, aided by his
easy and graceful style of delivery, produced a wonderful impression.
He said :

My Friends and Fellow-Citizens: I have very little to add to what
has been already said, and well said, upon the various topics suggested by
this occasion. In fact, I would gladly *escape* from saying anything, and
leave the remaining time to be occupied by addresses from other speakers.

When called upon to speak, however, I have always found it easier to
comply than to refuse ; more easy to find words than to fit my words to
the occasion ; and such is the case to-day. Centennial celebrations are
new things in American experience. I never attended one before. I am,
however, encouraged by the thought that when new things are attempted,
a certain degree of awkwardness is expected and excused. Thus far, I
believe, centennial celebrations have been monopolized by a few of our
oldest religious denominations. In their hands they have been found to
be not only very pleasant occasions, but very useful. They quicken zeal,
strengthen faith, and stimulate exertion. So deeply impressed with the
good effects of centennial celebrations are some of our colored brethren
that they think now of having one annually, and, it may be, quarterly.

Thus far, however, there is no formulated orthodox pattern for the
speeches to be made on such occasions, and each man is therefore left to
his own choice as to manner and matter.

One thing it will be in order to say here, at the outset : I am in favor of
centennial celebrations generally, and this Abolition Centennial particu-
larly. It is well to mark and observe the beginnings of great and important events in the history of society and civilization. All such occasions
can be made serviceable to human progress, welfare, and happiness.

I am glad, too, that this great and growing city of yours, the pride of
Pennsylvania, and perhaps the envy of some of its neighbors, is soon to
be the scene of a grand and memorable Centennial Celebration ; one that
will not only be metropolitan but national, and reflect glory upon our
country and upon the world. There is inspiration in the very thought of
such an assemblage. Here, on American soil, in this old city of the Declaration of Independence, will assemble the *elite* of all nations, kindreds,

tongues, and peoples. No argument is needed to prove that such a coming together will tend to liberality, peace, and brotherhood. Here, in this place, therefore, it is in order to bespeak the success of the grand Centennial which is to come after the one we are now holding. Our centennial celebration has attracted but little attention in comparison to that of next year; and yet I venture to claim for ours a higher, broader, and more sacred character than that which is to come after it. The Centennial of Seventy-Six stands for patriotism; ours stands for philanthropy. One stands for nationality; the other stands for universal humanity. [Applause.] One stands for what is transient; the other stands for what is permanent. Kingdoms, nationalities, principalities, powers, and republics, rise and fall; appear and vanish; but the great principles of liberty, justice, and humanity are unchangeable and eternal. [Renewed applause.] To participate in the celebration of a century of these principles is a sublime privilege. It is something of which a man may proudly tell his children, for it honorably associates his name with the grandest names and the noblest cause of modern history.

I rejoice to see on this platform, Lucretia Mott [applause,] Abby Kelly Foster [applause,] and the men and women, some of whom reached out to me a friendly hand years ago when I made my escape from slavery and came here to Philadelphia, and then to New England.

In listening to the discourse of our friend, Dr. Elder, this afternoon, I felt, as you did, that we had been fortunate in the selection of our historical orator. So far as the history of this society is concerned, he has swept the century and left but little for others to say.

While I am a man of the present, and feel deeply interested in the works of to-day, I have no sympathy with those who despise and neglect the origin of the anti-slavery movement and other movements among men of a kindred character. All *truth*, whether moral, physical or historical, is important, and may claim inspiration.

We talk of the dead past; but no part of the past is dead or indifferent to me. I rejoice in the full-grown man of anti-slavery, but I do not forget the cradle, nor the terrible struggles which have intervened—the periods of weakness and strength, of infancy and maturity.

I have somewhere seen a doubt expressed that there is any such thing as human progress. Some go so far as to say that this world is growing worse. To this view—this disheartening view, I may say—there is no more impressive contradiction than in the history of the anti-slavery cause. I know of no one period of the world's age for which I would be willing to exchange the present. There is no period in which the condi-

tions of existence were more easy and happy than now. Who amongst us
wants to go back to those great days of religious faith, when the Church
tore men's flesh from their bones with iron pincers, and roasted them alive
in fire and flame, because they entertained religious views different from
those proclaimed from its pulpit?

There are those who would tear men to-day, if they could, for a differ-
ence in religion. They call hard names and endeavor to excite prejudice ;
but we must all rejoice that the day of old-fashioned religious persecution
has now gone by. The day will come when persecution on account of
color will go the same way. No one can well doubt this when he looks
back over the history of the abolition movement, and observes and stu-
dies its gradual rise to power in the world. Doctrines of human liberty
which were deemed by the wise and prudent, radical, grotesque, and fa-
natical one hundred years ago, have come to be accepted as entirely
rational, wise, and beautiful in our day. As Lowell has it :

"Humanity sweeps onward :
    Where to-day the martyr stands,
    To-morrow crouches Judas,
    With the money in his hands."

I now hold in my hand a quaint and curious old volume, I will not say
of forgotten lore, for I think it is probably the only one of its kind now in
the United States. I have summoned it from the dust of nearly two hundred years to assist in this centennial celebration.

This venerable book was published in London, in the year of grace 1680 :
and is therefore nearly two hundred years old. It was presented to me
by Mr. John Gibson, in remembrance of my visit to White Haven, England, nearly thirty years ago. I thought it would be interesting on this
occasion for three reasons : First, because of its antiquity ; secondly, because it very strikingly illustrates the gradual dawn of anti-slavery truth
upon the world, and thirdly, because it is perhaps among the earliest of
those efforts of the human mind which have finally put an end to slavery
in most of this Western world.

The history of the book itself is significant and instructive. It was
written by a pious missionary of the Church of England, who had resi-
ded both in Virginia and in the West Indies, and of course, knew much
about the practical workings of slavery, both upon the slave and the
slave-master. In the production of this work of anti-slavery tendency he
does not seem to have been moved altogether by a benevolent thought or
purpose. His object was quite as much to shield the Church from oppro-

24

brium as to lift the down-trodden slave into manhood. In his introduction he gives this among other exciting causes of his writing. He says: "A petty reformer pamphlet was put into my hands by an officious *Friend* or *Quaker*, upon the perusal whereof I met with this malicious but crafty invection levelled against the ministers: " Who made you ministers of the Gospel to the white people only, and not to the tawnys and blacks also?" and he adds: " With many other of the like insolent queries." This proves that even at this early day the Quakers were in advance of their neighbors, and that they knew full well how to reprove the heartless injustice, partiality, and hypocrisy of the Church.

This book of the missionary, Morgan Godwin, designed to shield religion from the just reproaches of the friends of the slave, while it abounded in many excellent reflections, did not take very high ground. It was not a direct and conscious attack upon slavery. The idea that slavery in itself was wrong nowhere gets itself expressed in these pages. Mr. Godwin simply endeavored to prove that it was not a sin in the sight of God to baptize a negro and give him religious instruction ; and to show that these were not prejudicial to the right of the masters. But low as was this ground it was quite radical doctrine two hundred years ago. He asked neither freedom, citizenship, suffrage, nor equality for the negro. All he wanted was the right to put a little *religious* water upon him, and to save the poor fellow's soul.

He disposed of the black man in a very simple manner. He gave his body to the white man and his soul to the Lord. The right of the earthly master was as good to his part of the property as the right of the heavenly to his. But the black man himself had no right. When he looked for his body, that belonged to his master, and when he looked for his soul, that belonged to the Church ; and being unable to divide himself further, he did not have anything left for himself, and was, as we sometimes say in slang phrase, nowhere. From the elevated moral plane we now stand upon, it appears almost incredible that the negro's right to baptism and religious instruction was ever denied and resisted ; but such is the fact. We must remember that the gray light of morning is not the mid-day sun in its splendor, and that the age of Morgan Godwin was not the age of William L. Garrison, Gerrit Smith and Wendell Phillips.

Mr. Douglass gave some of the grounds of opposition to the baptism of the negro. It tended to increase his dignity and importance. It made him a Christian, and thus took him out of the category of heathenism from which the Bible permitted Christians to buy and hold slaves. It was alleged that a slave was not a fit subject for baptism. He was not a free moral agent—had no will of his own, and could not choose his own course in life. On any consistent theory of slavery the baptism of the negro was wrong and impolitic, and had a direct tendency to impair the value of the slave to his earthly master, and this was the view taken of the measure by the masters, and many and bloody have been the lashes laid on the backs of negroes for allowing themselves to be baptized

But something more than a glance at the past is due from us on this occasion. It is a glorious fact that slavery is abolished and the negro is enfranchised. A hundred years of labor have been rewarded by vast and wonderful progress. But he is an unwise reformer and unwise patriot who now considers his whole duty done and his work for freedom and country completed. No man of anti-slavery instincts can now look out upon the moral and political situation of this country without seeing danger to the results obtained by the immense labor and suffering of long years of agitation and of war and bloodshed. Every effort should now be made to save the results of this stupendous moral and physical contest.

It is said by some: "We have done enough for the negro." Yes, you have done a great deal for the negro, and, for one, I am deeply sensible of it, and grateful for it. But after all, what have you done? We were slaves—and you have made us free—and given us the ballot. But the world has never seen any people turned loose to such destitution as were the four million slaves of the South. The old roof was pulled down over their heads before they could make for themselves a shelter. They were free! free to hunger; free to the winds and rains of heaven; free to the pitiless wrath of enraged masters, who, since they could no longer control them, were willing to see them starve. They were free, without roofs to cover them. or bread to eat, or land to cultivate, and as a consequence died in such numbers as to awaken the hope of their enemies that they would soon disappear. We gave them freedom and famine at the same time. The marvel is that they still live. What the negro wants is, first, protection to the rights already conceded by law, and, secondly, education. Talk of having done enough for these people after two hundred years of enforced ignorance and stripes is absurd, cruel, and heartless.

Great was the statesmanship that gave the black man the ballot, but greater still will be the statesmanship that shall give him ample protection in exercising that sacred right, and education, and the knowledge to use his suffrage in such a manner as to preserve his own liberty and the highest welfare of the Government of this Republic. To-day, in the South, the school-house is burned. To-day, in Tennessee, Lucy Haydon is called from an inner room at midnight and shot down because she teaches colored children to read. To-day, in New Orleans and in Louisiana, and in parts of Alabama, the black man scarcely dares to deposit the votes which you gave him a right to deposit for fear of his life. We want your voices again; we want disinterested laborers as of old; we want Abby Kellys rising up in the wake of the Abby Kellys of other days; we want the Anna Dickinsons with a moral purpose to stir this country anew in behalf of humanity; we want to carry the standard, as the old Garrisonians carried it in 1840, outside of the Republican party, and outside of the Democratic party; we want this society to celebrate its second centennial, if need be.

Some of my friends in England used to send me money to help me publish my paper, and when slavery was abolished I was glad to send them word: '' I release you now, my friends, from sending me any more assistance, either for my paper or for the benefit of fugitive slaves.'' They wrote back: '' Douglass, we do not want to be released; we want you to go on; we want to help you.'' I say that we want this same spirit to take the field now in behalf of this race. We need you, my friends, almost as much as ever.

But I am here talking too long, and I will not detain you longer. I see here my friend and your friend—and you know he is here—Charles C. Burleigh [applause]; my friend Robert Purves [applause]; and other friends upon whom you can call. I know you want to hear as many voices as you can during the hour, and I thank you for the attention with which you have listened to my remarks.

Upon concluding, Mr. Douglass was the recipient of rounds of applause.

REMARKS BY LUCRETIA MOTT.

The chairman (Vice-President Wilson) then said:

On an occasion like this our hearts are full of tender memories. We are grateful to those whose voices, labors, and pens have advanced our cause. We are grateful to the private soldier who laid down his life in the storm of battle for the cause of the black man. We are grateful to the memory of Abraham Lincoln [applause], and we should not forget that this day is the tenth anniversary of his assassination. And among those to whom we should be grateful, our hearts should go out in gratitude to that noble class of American women who during the last forty years have worked and spoken for the cause. [Applause.] I propose now to present to you one of the most venerable and noble of the American women, whose voice for forty years has been heard and tenderly touched many noble hearts. Age has dimmed her eye and weakened her voice, but her heart, like the heart of a wise man and a wise woman, is yet young. I present to you Lucretia Mott.

[This announcement was greeted with renewed manifestations of welcome.]

Lucretia Mott, upon coming forward, said :

I came here without the least expectation of saying a word, understanding the meeting to be at the call of the Society for Promoting the Abolition of Slavery, as organized long before the Anti-Slavery Society, headed by William Lloyd Garrison. In this, the first society, women were not expected to take part. I therefore, should feel very much out of place were there not a union at this time of both societies. Then again, owing to a severe cold, my hoarseness is such that I cannot be heard probably many feet from me; but my interest in this cause makes me willing, at the suggestion of your chairman, to occupy a few moments

The speaker, after expressing the hope that what had been said would have the effect to stimulate her hearers to greater zeal in the support of schools for the education of people of color, and in the many similar directions in which they had been engaged, proceeded to correct an erroneous statement that Elizabeth Heyrick was a member of the Society of Friends.

Referring to what had been said concerning the gratitude of the negro, she gave some instances from her personal experience, and remarked that much yet remained to be done in order to put a stop to outrages upon the colored people such as were still perpetrated in the South. She referred to the moral influence of the anti-slavery sentiments in bringing about the emancipation of the colored race.

The next exercise was the rendition by the Hutchinson Family of the verses beginning :

> " It is coming up the steep of time,
> And this whole world is growing brighter."

REMARKS OF CHARLES C. BURLEIGH.

The chairman then introduced the next speaker in these words: " I now present Charles C. Burleigh, who gave youth, talent, and courage to the cause."

Mr. Burleigh came forward and said :

I see that this platform is draped with the stars and stripes of the

Union, and in that I see one signal token of the change that has been wrought in this country by the proclamation of anti-slavery truth ; for now there is nothing in that emblem to cause an anti-slavery meeting to shrink from it. The time was when this flag floated over four millions of slaves and, under it, the military power of the nation stood pledged to keep those slaves in bondage. To-day the military power of the nation stands pledged to defend the right of the emancipated slave not only to be a man but to be a co-sovereign of the Republic, and to share with the proudest of his white brethren in the exercise of all the rights which belong to the citizen of this great Republic.

We are celebrating the one-hundredth anniversary of a society, but for whose existence, with that of similar organizations, it would have been impossible for this nation, without exposing itself to taunts and reproaches, to celebrate the centennial anniversary of its freedom in the presence of the nations of the earth. We can now stand as a free people in the presence of other nations, and will not hear the reproach that over this land a bastard Freedom waves her fustian flag in mockery over slaves. Something therefore has been achieved by this society, not merely for the raising up of the chattel to the condition of a man, and the man to the condition of a co-sovereign, but for the entire nation and for the progress of humanity.

The speaker went on to argue that in all this the might of the truth, which was the agency whereby the victory was achieved, was plainly visible. This truth had been mighty, not only in enlisting men under the banner of an unpopular cause, and strengthening them to cast behind ease and interest, and honor and reputation, and stand in the fore-front of the battle against outrage and persecution, but in constraining even the enemies of the cause to do its service, and its adversaries to accomplish its work. In rebelling against the Government, and making slavery the corner-stone of the empire, the slave power not only forced upon the nation the necessity of crushing rebellion in order to save itself, but it robbed itself of the shield behind which it had sheltered through all the preceding years. It could no longer plead its constitutional or legal rights after it had risen in rebellion against the very authority under which it claimed to exercise its guarantees of protection. The speaker argued in proof of his position that the truth proclaimed by the anti-slavery champions of the country had not only rallied around it the friends of justice and humanity, but had converted their enemies into instruments for achieving its own victories.

REMARKS OF ROBERT PURVIS, Esq.

Mr. Purvis, referring to the chairman's notice that the meeting would adjourn to re assemble at Bethel church in the evening, said it was doubtful whether Vice-President Wilson would be present then, and added: " I wish to say, yielding to the impulse of the instant, and as the certain representative of millions in the country, that we are more indebted to the able chairman and to his distinguished colleague who now enjoys his reward in Heaven, than to any men in the national councils for all that now enables the colored race to feel that they have a country to love, and a flag which they can conscientiously honor and defend."

The remarks were received with applause. Bishop Campbell pronounced the benediction and the meeting adjourned to Bethel church at 7½ o'clock.

THE EVENING EXERCISES.

The Centennial celebration was continued according to adjournment, at Bethel Methodist Episcopal Church, Sixth above Lombard. A large audience were gathered before the hour. There were on the platform, Vice President Wilson, Frederick Douglas, Bishop Campbell, C. C. Burleigh, Mrs. F. E. W. Harper, Rev. G. H. Ball, of New York, Rev. J. W. Dungee of Richmond, Va, Prof. J. M. Langston, John Oliver of Richmond, Va, and others. Bishop Campbell, presiding, desired Rev. Dr Ball to ask a blessing. The Hutchinson Family sang. A letter from Bishop D. A. Payne was read, encouraging the Society not to desist from their efforts until Slavery no longer existed anywhere. Mrs. F. E. W. Harper was introduced. She said :

The great problem to be solved by the American people, if I understand it, is this— whether or not there is strength enough in democracy, virtue enough in our civilization, and power enough in our religion to have mercy and deal justly with four millions of people but lately translated from the old oligarchy of slavery to the new commonwealth of freedom : and upon the right solution of this question depends in a large measure the future strength, progress, and durability of our nation.   The most important question before us colored people is not simply what the Democratic party may do against us or the Republican party do for us; but what are we going to do for ourselves? What shall we do towards developing our character, adding our quota to the civilization and strength of the country, diversifying our industry, and practicing those lordly virtues that conquer success, and turn the world's dread laugh into admiring recognition? The white race have yet work to do in making practical the political axiom of equal rights, and the Christian idea of human brotherhood ; but while I lift mine eyes to the future I would not ungratefully ignore the past. One hundred years ago and Africa was the privileged hunting-ground of Europe and America, and the flag of different nations hung a sign of death on the coasts of Congo and Guinea, and for years unbroken silence had hung around the horrors of the African slave trade. Since then Great Britain and other nations have wiped the bloody traffic from their hands, and shaken the gory merchandise from their fingers, and the brand of piracy has been placed upon the African slave trade. Less than fifty years ago mob violence belched out its wrath against the men who dared to arraign the slaveholder before the bar of conscience and Christendom. Instead of golden showers upon his head, he who garrisoned the front had a halter around his neck. Since, if I may borrow the idea, the nation has caught the old inspiration from his lips and written it in the new organic world. Less than twenty-five years ago slavery clasped hands with King Cotton, and said slavery fights and cotton conquers for American slavery. Since then slavery is dead, the colored man has exchanged the fetters on his wrist for the ballot in his hand. Freedom is king and Cotton a subject.

It may not seem to be a gracious thing to mingle complaint in a season of general rejoicing. It may appear like the ancient Egyptians seating a corpse at their festal board to avenge the Americans for their short-comings when so much has been accomplished. And yet with all the victories and triumphs which freedom and justice have won in this country, I do not believe there is another civilized nation under Heaven where there are half so many people who have been brutally and shamefully murdered, with or without impunity, as in this republic within the last ten years. And who cares? Where is the public opinion that has scorched with red-hot indignation the cowardly murderers of Vicksburgh and Louisiana ? Sheridan lifts up the vail from Southern society, and behind it is the smell of blood, and our bones scattered at the grave's mouth ; murdered people ; a White League with its "covenant of death and agreement with hell." And who cares? What city pauses one hour to drop a pitying tear over these mangled corpses, or has forged against the perpetrator one thunderbolt of furious protest? But let there be a supposed or real invasion of Southern rights by our soldiers, and our great commercial emporium will rally its forces from the old man in his classic shades, to clasp hands with "Dead Rabbits" and " Plug-uglies" in protesting against military interference. What we need to-day in the onward march of humanity is a public sentiment in favor of common justice and simple mercy. We have a civilization which has produced grand and magnificent results, diffused knowledge, overthrown slavery, made constant conquests over nature, and built up a wonderful material prosperity. But two things are wanting in American civilization—a keener and deeper, broader and tenderer sense of justice—a sense of humanity, which shall crystalize into the life of the nation the sentiment that justice, simple justice, is the right, not simply of the strong and powerful, but of the weakest and feeblest of all God's children ; a deeper and broader humanity, which will teach men to look upon their feeble brethren not as vermin to be crushed out, or beasts of burden to be bridled and bitted, but as the children of the living God ; of that God whom we may earnestly hope is in perfect wisdom and in perfect love working for the best good of all. Ethnologists may differ about the origin of the human race. Huxley may search for it in protoplasms, and Darwin send for the missing links, but there is one thing of which we may rest assured ; that we all come from the living God and that He is the common Father. The nation that has no reverence for man is also lacking in reverence for God and needs to be instructed. As fellow-citizens, leaving out all humanitarian views—as a mere matter of political economy it is better to have the colored race a living force animated and strengthened by self-reliance and self-respect, than a stagnant mass, degraded and self-condemned. Instead of the North relaxing its efforts to diffuse education in the South, it behooves us for our national life, to throw into the South all the healthful reconstructing influences we can command. Our work in this country is grandly constructive. Some races have come into this world and overthrown and destroyed. But if it is glory to destroy, it is happiness to save ; and Oh ! what a noble work there is before our nation ! Where is there a young man who would consent to lead an aimless life when there are such glorious opportunities before him ? Before our young men is another battle—not a battle of flashing swords and clashing steel—but a moral warfare, a battle against ignorance, poverty, and low social condition. In physical warfare the keenest swords may be blunted and the loudest batteries hushed; but in the great conflict of moral and spiritual progress your weapons shall be brighter for their service and better for their use. In fighting truly and nobly for others you win the victory for yourselves.

Give power and significance to your own life, and in the great work of upbuilding there is room for woman's work and woman's heart. Oh, that our hearts were alive and our vision quickened, to see the grandeur of the work that lies before. We have some culture among us, but I think our culture lacks enthusiasm. We need a deep earnestness and a lofty unselfishness to round out our lives. It is the inner life that develops the outer, and if we are in earnest the precious things lie all around our feet, and we need not waste our strength in striving after the dim and unattainable. Woman, in your golden youth; mother, binding around your heart all the precious ties of life,—let no magnificence of culture, or amplitude of fortune, or refinement of sensibilities, repel you from helping the weaker and less favored. If you have ampler gifts, hold them as larger opportunities with which you can benefit others. Oh, it is better to feel that the weaker and feebler our race the closer we will cling to them than it is to isolate ourselves from them in selfish, or careless unconcern, saying there is a lion without. Inviting you to this work I do not promise you fair sailing and unclouded skies. You may meet with coolness where you expect sympathy; disappointment where you feel sure of success; isolation and loneliness instead of heart-support and co-operation. But if your lives are based and built upon these divine certitudes, which are the only enduring strength of humanity, then whatever defeat and discomfiture may overshadow your plans or frustrate your schemes, for a life that is in harmony with God and sympathy for man there is no such word as fail. And in conclusion, permit me to say, let no misfortunes crush you; no hostility of enemies or failure of friends discourage you. Apparent failure may hold in its rough shell the germs of a success that will blossom in time, and bear fruit throughout eternity. What seemed to be a failure around the Cross of Calvary and in the garden, has been the grandest recorded success.

Elizur Wright was then introduced. He said :—

I have noticed that Elizur Wright, *junior*, has been announced as one of the speakers on this occasion. No such person is now in existence, and there has not been in twenty years. I remember there was one, and how, with his young wife and child, he came to this city in 1803 to attend the formation of a new anti-slavery society, a sort of junior to the one whose birth is to-day celebrated. He then related the occurrence of a grand dinner in this city, at which his wife felt honored at being led to the table by a sea captain who was colored.

There is in all society an upper and a lower stratum. But they are not regulated by color or nationality. The distinction belongs to character and culture.

Mr. Wright then adverted to the Civil-Rights Bill, which he said would meet no trouble in the South. Two years ago he took a journey through the South, and the best car on a train on which he rode was half filled with negroes—well-dressed, fine-appearing—and the white people who sat in the car did not feel at all disgraced. It is true there are, in low society, cases of outrage, but they are the exception. The civil-rights bill will go into effect.

After urging the duty of the coming generation to work for the elevation and complete freedom of the African race, Mr. Wright read two paragraphs describing a discussion in Green-street Church, Boston, in 1833, between a Mr. Findlay and the speaker, the three questions of which were: Whether the colonization of the negroes was not beneficial to the Africans? Whether it does not tend to encourage slavery? and whether the only hope for the abolition of slavery does not lie in propagating the doctrine of immediate emancipation?

At the conclusion of Mr. Wright's remarks, Mr. Purvis said: "that in this very Bethel church in 1817, the first protest was made against the colonization scheme, and his honored father-in-law presided on that occasion."

Professor John M. Langston was introduced. He commenced by remarking that he could hardly understand why he should have been honored by an invitation to attend so grand a commemoration. He had no merits and had performed no work that justified him in intruding upon their patience. And yet he would not represent the class whose representative he was unless, in their name, he testified to the inestimable debt of gratitude that is owed by them and will be owed by their posterity—by the whole population of the Union, regardless of race, of learning, of condition; by the population of the world, annually holding its way more in accordance with the principles of freedom, of general education and popular government and so with more and higher success,—the great debt of gratitude that is owed by all now living in this country and by many in other lands, and that will be due from men every year, to the PENNSYLVANIA ABOLITION SOCIETY for their staunch efforts in securing universal freedom. (Applause).

3

The history of the Association, owing to its objects and achievements, sweep in an interest that is not confined to any class: an interest that is not confined to any people, and whose scope and consequences cannot be foretold by human inspiration. It affects the emancipation of a whole race; and in that it touches the progress and character of all who are brought in contact with that race, the forms of government over the world and the world's progress in all departments. There was a recent time in American history when no man in all its length and breadth, could read the Declaration of Independence and say that he possessed all of his civil and political liberties. Garrison could not speak in New Orleans, nor could the silver-tongued Phillips address an audience south of Mason and Dixon's line. Nor was it expedient for John C. Calhoun to address his arguments in Independence Hall, or for Davis and Yulee and Mason to propound theirs in Faneuil Hall. Speech was itself in thrall, and bound to the section in which it found voice. When Garrison and Phillips had been invited to speak in Cincinnati, they were counseled by their friends not to do so. There was danger that the mobs of Covington and Cincinnati would assassinate them publicly; and it is notorious that the opposing arguments that reached Washington from the North and from the South, advanced no further in either direction. This impugned and belied the very freedom declared in the Declaration and Constitution; and made both the mockery of Europe. The contradiction is reconciled; the taunt is silenced; speech is legally free and protected over all the Union and the Pennsylvania Abolition Society have done more than any other agency— more than all other agencies combined 'to vitalize the Constitution and give being to the Declaration. This society fought for the glowing assertion of all the centuries, that mankind are born free and equal and are endowed with inalienable right to life, liberty and the pursuit of happiness. They kept the contrast between the declaration and its practice in a clear light. They repeated the assertion and reasserted it. They argued the justice with the very facts and reasons that had been presented to the Congress by whom the Declaration was framed. Undisturbed by ridicule, unchecked by hostility, undaunted by persecution, they kept the law in the van of the fight; they sustained it by reserves of humane reason; by appeals to national strength and welfare, and growth, and influence, and wealth; they disseminated the truth in churches, at the polls, in lyceums, by the press; they were unanswerable because their claim was founded in equity, and recognized in religion, and had ineradicable place in the great muniment of national being. They appealed to the individual conscience as well as to pride, patriotism, piety and interest, and they won, and now celebrate a victory immeasurably greater than that of Yorktown or Waterloo or Marathon. Those were the victories of nation over nation, or at the utmost of a principle of limited application. We celebrate the successful battle of the grandest principle in human organization ; that is confined to no race, limited to no country, cramped by no restriction, but is as broad as the world, as applicable as humanity itself and as enduring as time. The sentiment which elected Abraham Lincoln was contained in an address delivered before the Pennsylvania Abolition Society by Benjamin Rush, one of its earliest and most honored members. It was : " Freedom and Slavery cannot long exist together ! " (Applause).

Ladies and Gentlemen of the Abolition Society ! Those who see the American citizens of African descent one hundred years hence, will be proud of them, and convinced that the great century struggle that won their enfranchisement was worth infinitely more than it cost. We are now leaving politics. We have gained through them the rights and opportunities they conferred, that could be secured in no other way. We are devoting ourselves to learning and industry ; the attainment of wealth and manufacture of character. We shall never leave our home. There are but two facts to be recognized. We are here. The White race are here. Both share the same rights ; make and obey the same laws ; struggle for progress under the same conditions. The logical conclusion of our birthright and of our proclaimed and perfected equality before the law is that we shall remain, and remaining strive with equal advantages with our white fellow-citizens for our own good and the nation's welfare.

Prof. Langston's speech was received with great applause.

Abby Kelley Foster said that she did not intend to make a speech, for she could not. She merely wished to congratulate the Society on its grand work in lifting up the oppressed and down-trodden. The American Abolition Society and its hundreds of branches died when they had seen the political disabilities of the colored race removed, and the Pennsylvania Society is the only one now existing.

Henry Wilson, Vice President of the United States, was introduced. One word he said of many expressed during the session met his most hearty response. It was that which called the people to prepare to sustain the government of which they are now a part. For more than two years there has been much said about public men being a commodity. They are criticised for every act and the vilest motives are assigned for all they do or refuse to do. Now for twenty years at least, the public men of this country have been far ahead of the average of those whom they represent ; and they are so still. The slave power in this country did not go down because the popular demand had changed. When the rebellion broke out, a great majority of the people of the country were not anti-slavery in their feelings and were very far from being abolitionists. There were however among them those who enlightened, formed and directed sentiment.

The review of only a few months shows by the losses how many great men have been taken from our ranks. Within the last thirty months William H. Seward, who rendered incalculable service in behalf of emancipation, has been taken away. Chief Justice Chase, who rendered great and grand services notwithstanding some mistakes, has gone too. Horace Greeley, whose services to the cause through his influential journal cannot be overestimated, has gone. Gone too is Charles Sumner, who defended the same cause with unsurpassed eloquence ; and gone because he defended it. Gerritt Smith, associated with the struggle from its birth and untiring and resolute in sheltering it, has gone. And so has Abraham Lincoln, in whom all purpose and all desire concentrated for a supreme effort, and through whom they won their whole demand. And Lincoln and Sumner and Seward paid with their lives for their advocacy.

Let us now, succeeding these pioneers, emulate their conduct and discharge our different duties as resolutely and wisely and perseveringly. Let us step to the very verge to raise, improve and elevate the colored men of America, whether they are in the North or the South. This is our duty, and is doubly urgent owing to what our predecessors and companions have won. We start with the determination that the colored race shall have all and the same rights and privileges that the white enjoy. We start with the determination that the millions of whites who were kept in ignorance and poverty and subjection equal to slavery, from the Delaware to the Rio Grande, because the colored were slaves, shall be educated and enfranchised. Slavery is dead, but its consequences are not dead, and must be wholly vanquished. We are to conquer these as we did their seed. We must struggle for education. We must create free schools for white and black in all of the South and everywhere. True policy requires us to assist in rebuilding the broken industries of the South. In a purely Christian spirit we must maintain that equal rights belong to all American citizens, and that any opposition is as treasonable to republican government as advocating a monarchy. We must animate, vitalize and enforce all that we have added to the Constitution, and give it efficacy as extensive as that. We must change wrong opinions. We must concede what can be conceded, generously. We must hold to and defend the essentials with a firmness that will not surrender even the shadow of right and justice.

Vice President Wilson's speech was received with frequent applause and applause followed it.

Frederick Douglass succeeded Mr. Wilson. He paid a glowing eulogy to Abraham Lincoln and divided it with Henry Wilson. He also touched briefly upon the issues of the recent elections in Connecticut and New Hampshire, as they concerned the social equality of the races. His conclusion was that as the negro procured freedom from political necessity, so he must procure education for social necessity. He was followed by Robert Purves in a few extemporaneous remarks that criticised the republican party for having neglected to keep the promises made in 1872 and only offered a substitute that is inefficient and worthless. The Hutchinson Family sang, and the long exercises of the evening, patiently followed by a great assemblage who testified their interest by their attention and their appreciation by their applause, were ended with the benediction.

Another celebration speedily follows this. Its lights are seen, its music is heard, its approach is near. It will collect all the races of all the States; all the records, and attainments and hopes of all Americans, in its great embrace. It will draw contributions and representatives and spectators from every nation on earth; and will go out in its effects as far, and for all time to commend the uses of free government. That includes the celebration of the Pennsylvania Abolition Society as a constituent. And no constituent is more mighty. It brought back the administration of the nation to harmony with the national constitution. It made the constitution operative. It accomplished the freedom that is necessary for American being and doing: it unlocked the door to finer humanities and greater progress for all everywhere. It turned out and locked out the barbarism of slavery from the civilization of the century and of the world. The celebration whose record is closed was not marred by the abuse of the old slave-holders nor by partizan feeling. There were no untimely or inappropriate demands made. The kindest feelings of a great jubilee reigned supreme and penetrated the whole; and the occasion was employed to impress the need of education, of virtue, of industry, of all the virtues that make a nation's greatness and retain it. It was in spirit, in character and in every particular as great and brilliant a contribution as any the Centennial will hold, and there can be no display than that will not radiate new light from the colors of this anniversary.

CONCLUSION.

Such in its motives; such in its membership; such in its pacific and lawful and philanthropic labors; such in its hopes and failures, in its counsels and trials, was the Abolition Society of the United States. It was organized when the political independence of the nation had just been won, and all men rejoiced in political freedom. It was organized with the co-operation of Franklin, and the countenance of his most eminent co-temporaries. It formulated an eternal truth that had been incorporated in the immortal declaration, that "All men are born free and equal, and endowed with inalienable rights." It had European countenance, and through all its century of alternating hope and depression, and in the very instant of apparent final defeat, it had the consciences of mankind sub-scribing its truth and justice.

The bloodshed of an unprovoked and wanton civil war preceded its final success, and its victory was hallowed by the murder of that martyr President, whose great Proclamation broke every shackle and freed every slave. The victory surged forward beyond any dream of the most visionary at the beginning. The victims of more than a century of slavery, telling their numbers by millions, were not only freed but enfranchised. Their gallant conduct in the field through the war; their self-sacrificing and constant support in civil life; the order, the industry, the charity, the tolerance they showed in all situations, and their zeal for learning and active labors, commanded the great Constitutional Amendment, by which the freedmen were made citizens, and invested with all the rights and all the responsibilities of their white fellow-citizens. The Centennial of the Abolition Society thus celebrated the abolition of the slaves; the proof that they deserved for personal and patriotic merit what they received through political justice, invoked by the rebellion of their former masters. And it was brightened by the great efforts that have been and are being made by these new citizens in every State, to educate themselves and their children, to maintain schools, to erect churches; to acquire property, and command through desert, the equal esteem of all classes, and the same social and political standing, irrespective of color, that the African race have in France.

The Centennial was made more august by similar consequences, indirectly won through its labors, in other lands. At the very instant when, starting in and from the great attempt of this society here, slavery was outlawed in the Union; Russia put an end to serfdom in her lands; and Spain moderated her rigor in Porto Rico; and white and black fought together for independence in Cuba; and Brazil declared a system of gradual emancipation, and human bondage over all the world was limited to a few countries, with evidence of its early and total suppression. The light and warmth that irradiated the celebration, perfect in tone and pervasive and unqualified as they were, from all parts of the Union, were augmented from all parts of the world; and it was possible to apprehend the highest elevation of citizens of African descent in the United States, lately slaves, concurrently with the spread of emancipation to the African and other races, in every portion of the world, and the absolute reign of freedom for the first time in the world's history.

Such, so brilliant and so great in its history and direct and consequential attainments was the Abolition Society. It contained as pure, and intelligent, and earnest, and pious souls as any society ever had. It won a great fight against the greatest odds. It transmitted its uses to other lands, and saw them succeeding. And it wisely employed the instant of victory, to plan new and nobler labors for the elevation of those to whom it gave freedom. This is the work devolved upon the shoulders of these members who live, and the children of members who have their reward. The political power of the Union, its theory of government, and the necessities of every State, require a general assistance for this labor, that has been partly given. The next Centennial will be national and unopposed, and hearty—when the descendants of the late slaves are no longer freedmen—but fully clothed with every attribute of manhood, and invested with all the rights and considerations of citizenship.

SCHOOLS AT THE FOLLOWING PLACES.

Whilst the Society has felt the deepest interest in the educational work, means have not been so abundant as to enable them to respond to the pressing claims of Schools and Colleges, further than now and then a case. Aid, however, has been extended to some extent to the following schools and colleges embraced in the subjoined list.

Waterford, Va.
Janesville, N. C.
Mount Pisgah, Md.
Woodlawn, Va.
St. Mary's, Pa.
Rikersville, S. C.
Gum Springs, Va.
Gainsville, S. C.
Bidwell, "
Lenairs, "
Falls Church, Va.
Waldo, "
Manassas, "
Lively Oak, "
Fairfield, "
Goldsboro', N. C.
Beaufort, S. C.
Heathsville, Va.
Sumpter, S. C.
Jacksonville, Fla.
Laurel Factory, Md.
Blackville, S. C.
Frogmore, "
St. Helena, "
Midway, "
Camden, N. J.
Mount Pleasant, S. C.
Columbia, Ga.
Chambersburg, Pa.
Richmond, Va.
Leesburg, "

Clark's Chapel, Ga.
Alexandria, Va.
Centreville, "
Warren, "
Sharpsburg, Md.
Painter's Post, Va.
Brentsville, "
Ship's Island, Miss.
Grand View, Va.
Oberlin, Ohio.
Broad Mountain, Va.
Milford, Del.
Barnwell, S. C.
Howard University, D. C.
Wilberforce " Ohio.
Hampton Institute, Va.
Albany " Ohio.
Maryville, " Tenn.
Bridgewater Orphans' School, Pa.
Maylandville " " "
Colored Orphans' Home, D. C.
Orphan Home, S. C.
Moral Reform Home, N. J.
Brown St. Public School, Pa.
Bethany " " "
Race St. Friends' Freedmen's Association, Pa.
Arch " " " " "
C. S. Schaeffer's Mission, Va.
Penna. Freedmen's Ass'n, Pa.
Several Students at Lincoln University.

AN ACT

TO INCORPORATE A SOCIETY.

BY THE NAME OF

THE PENNSYLVANIA SOCIETY

FOR

Promoting the Abolition of Slavery, and for the Relief of Free Negroes unlawfully held in bondage, and for improving the condition of the African Race.

———————•———————

SECTION 1. Whereas, a voluntary Society has for some years subsisted in this State, by the name and title of "The Pennsylvania Society for Promoting the Abolition of Slavery, and the Relief of Free Negroes unlawfully held in Bondage," which has evidently co-operated with the views of the Legislature, expressed in the act of the General Assembly of this Commonwealth, passed the first day of March, in the year of our Lord, one thousand seven hundred and eighty, entitled "An Act for the gradual abolition of slavery," and a supplement thereto, passed the twenty-ninth day of March, in the year of our Lord one thousand seven hundred and eighty-eight, entitled "An Act to explain and amend an act, entitled an act for the gradual abolition of slavery;"

And whereas, this said Society have lately extended their plan so far as to comprehend within their intentions the improving the condition as well of those negroes who now are, or hereafter shall become free, by the operation of the said acts, or otherwise, and their posterity; and have, by their petition to this House, prayed to be created and erected into a body politic and corporate, for the purpose of increasing their ability to be useful in the several matters aforesaid.

SECTION 2. *Be it therefore enacted, and it is hereby enacted, by represent-*
atives of the freemen of the Commonwealth of Pennsylvania, in General As-
sembly met, and by the authority of the same, That the present members of
the said Society, viz.

Dr. Benjamin Franklin, James Pemberton, Jonathan Penrose, Thomas
Harrison, James Starr, William Lippincott, John Thomas, Benjamin
Hornor, Samuel Richards, John Evans, John Todd, James Whiteall,
Edward Brooks, Thomas Armat, John Warner, Samuel Davis, Thomas
Bartow, Robert Evans, Robert Wood, Seymour Hart, Richard Hum-
phreys, Robert Towers, Joseph Moore, Joseph Russell, William Zane,
Israel Whelen, Samuel Baker, Richard Price, Charles Jervis, Israel
Hallowell, Clement Biddle, Amos Wickersham, Pattison Hartshorne,
Nathan Sellers, David Sellers, Isaac Parrish, Zachariah Jess, Dr. Ben-
jamin Rush, John Field, Richard Jones, William Poyntell, Andrew
Carson, Philip Price, John Hunt, junr., Norris Jones, John Morton,
Thomas Penrose, Thomas Poultney, Thomas Eddy, Isaac Weaver, jun.,
Caleb Attmore, Joseph Budd, Abraham Sharpless, Isaac Massey, James
Lewis, Thomas Shoemaker, Robert Morris, Jeremiah Paul, Thomas Savery,
Francis Bailey, Thomas Shields, George Eddy, John Morrison, John
Morris, Joseph Clark, Zachariah Poulson, junr., Thomas Parker, William
Graham, Thomas Rogers, John Poultney, Isaac Bonsall, Joseph Cruk-
shank, John Jacobs, Nathan Boys, William Ashby, Jacob Trasel, William
Jackson, Charles Crawford, Ellis Yarnall, John Olden, Tench Coxe,
Jonathan Pugh, John Reece, Jacob Shoemaker, junr, William M'Ilhen-
ney, Caleb Lownes, John Letchworth, William West, Isaac Pearson,
Burton Wallace, Francis Johnson, Joseph Sharpless, Thomas Wistar,
Joseph Lownes, Benjamin Say, Joseph Anthony, Caspar W. Haines,
Joseph Bacon, George Rutter, David Lownes, Bartholomew Wistar,
George Fox, William T. Franklin, William Rawle, James Trenchard,
Conrad Hanse, Samuel Coates, Richard Wells, Sharp Delany, Jonathan
Willis, junr., Joseph Gibbons, Samuel Pancoast, Kearney Wharton, Dr.
James Hutchinson, Charles Williams, John Claypoole, John Dowers,
Hilary Baker, George Latimer, Andrew Geyer, James Read, Peter
Woglom, John Kaign, John Todd, junr., Philip Benezet, Joseph James,
Dr. Caspar Wistar, Dr. Samuel P. Griffitts, Thomas Fitzgerald, Stephen
Maxfield, Philip Price, junr., Israel Pleasants, Mordecai Churchman,
Thomas Annesly, Benjamin W. Morris, John M'Cree, George Richie,
James Olden, John Hutchinson, George Wilson, Jacob Parke, Thomas
Lawrence, Dr. John Foulke, Jesse Waterman, James Trimble, Dr. Wil-
liam Rogers, Dr. Nicholas Collin, Samuel M. Fox, Benjamin Shoemaker,
Joseph P. Norris, George Roberts, Jeremiah Parker, Abraham Liddon,
John Bleakley, Joseph Inskeep, Robert Waln, Richard Parker, John
Starr, Nathan Allen Smith, Thomas Norton, Robert Taggart, Samuel
Emlen, junr., William Kid, Dr. John Andrews, Zebulon Potts, Samuel
Kinsby, Nathan Field, Daniel Trotter, Benjamin Taylor, James Smith,
junr., Caleb Carmalt, Robert Roberts, William Chancellor, Thomas For-
rest, Jonathan Jones, Ebenezer Breed, George Aston, Thomas Proctor,
George Davis, John Smilie, Thomas Palmer, Anthony Felix Wuibert,

Matthew Hale, Richard Peters, Joseph Thomas, Thomas Ross, Isaac Buckbee, Joshua Gilpin, Dr. Amos Gregg, Girard Vogels, Richard Riley, Samuel Claphamson, Zaccheus Collins, Henry Hale Grayham, John Ely, Richard H. Morris, John Staplir, junr., Daniel May, Andrew Johnston, S. Barnett, William Welsh, Isaiah Harr, Charles Lukins, James Smith, J. Morris, Ambrose Updegraff, Peter Mondirf, Thomas Fisher, Robert Kammersly, John Smith, William Webb, John Roberts, John Kittera, William Brisband, William Gibbons, Samuel Updegraff, Caleb Johnson, Robert Verree, Dr. John Chapman, Alexander Addison, Samuel Redwood, Rees Cadwallader, Samuel Jackson, Dr. John Luther, Dr. John Story, Benjamin Wright and Eli Lewis, all of the State of Pennsylvania;

And Joseph Shottwell, junr., David Cooper, Samuel Allison, Thomas Redman, Thomas Stokes, John Wistar, Thomas Clements, Joseph Sloan, Ebenezer Howel, Clement Hall, James Jess, Benjamin Wright, Richard Waln, Stacy Biddle, Hezekiah Hughes, Thomas Githen, all of the State of New Jersey;

The honorable John Jay, and Matthew Clarkson, of the State of New York;

John Boggs, Caleb Kirk, and Warner Mifflin, of the State of Delaware;

Zebulon Hollingsworth, John Richardson, Woolman Hickson, John Feigle, Joseph Wilkinson, and John Needles, of the State of Maryland;

Samuel Hopkins, Benjamin Forster, Enos Hitchcock, Benjamin West, Moses Brown, William Patton, Samuel Vinson, Thomas Robinson, and Jonathan Easton, of the State of Rhode Island;

John Saunders, George Tegal, and George Corbyn, of the State of Virginia;

Noah Webster, Thomas Gain, and Benjamin West, of the State of Massachusetts;

Capel Loft, David Barclay, Granville Sharp, Dr. Richard Price, James Phillips, Thomas Day, Dr. Thomas Clarkson, the right Hon. William Pitt, Dr. John Coakley Lettsom, William Dillwyn, Robert Robinson, and William Hollick, of the Kingdom of Great Britain;

L'Abbe Raynal, Le Marquis de la Fayette, J. P. Brissot de Warville, Charton de Terriere, and Francis Clery du Pont, of the Kingdom of France;

And such other person and persons as shall be hereafter elected and chosen in the manner hereinafter mentioned, and their successors, be and they are hereby created and declared to be one body politic and corporate in deed and in law, by the name, style and title of "The Pennsylvania Society for Promoting the Abolition of Slavery, and for the Relief of Free Negroes unlawfully held in Bondage, and for improving the condition of the African Race," and by the same name shall have perpetual succession, and shall be able to sue and to be sued, implead, and be answered unto in all courts of law and equity, and to make, have and use one common seal to give authenticity to their acts, deeds, records and proceedings, and the same at their pleasure to break, alter, change and make anew, and to purchase, take and hold by gift, grant, demise, bargain and sale, will and devise, bequest, testament, legacy, or by any other mode of conveyance, any lands, tenements, goods, chattels, or estate, real, personal or mixed, or choses in action, not exceeding at any one time the yearly value of fifteen hundred pounds lawful money of Pennsylvania in the whole ; and the same to give, grant, bargain, sell, demise, convey and assure to others, for the whole or any lesser estate than they have in the same, in such manner and form as the said Society at their future meetings hereinafter described shall order and direct ; and to apply the rents, issues, and profits, income and interest of such estate, and the monies arising from the sales of any parts thereof, to the uses, ends, intents and purposes of their institution, according to the rules, orders, regulations, and constitution of the said Society, now in force, or which, according to the provisions hereinafter made, shall from time to time be declared and ordained, touching and concerning the same, as fully and effectually as any natural person or body politic and corporate within this State, by the constitution and laws of this commonwealth, can do, and perform the like things.

SECTION 3. *And be it further enacted, and it is hereby enacted by the authority aforesaid,* That the officers of the said Society shall consist of one President, two Vice-presidents, two Secretaries, one Treasurer, who shall also be the keeper of the common seal, and so many counsellors as the said Society shall from time to time think proper to appoint and elect, all of whom shall be chosen annually by ballot of a majority of votes of the whole number of members who shall be present at the quarterly meeting hereinafter mentioned, which shall be held on the first second day of the week (called Monday) in the first month (called January) in every year after the passing of this act, or at such other time, and at such place, as the said Society shall, by their rules and orders, direct and appoint ; and of such committees, for carrying into execution the designs of the said institution, as the said Society heretofore have appointed, and hereafter at any of their quarterly or special meetings shall agree to, and appoint in the manner and form to be hereafter agreed upon.

SECTION 4. *And be it further enacted by the authority aforesaid,* That the said society shall and may hold four quarterly meetings in every year, at such place and hour of the day as they shall agree unto, on every the first second day of the week (called Monday) in every the first, fourth, seventh and tenth months, called January, April, July, and October, in every year forever hereafter, and may adjourn the said quarterly meetings from time to time ; and shall and may hold such other special meetings as the Society by their rules and orders shall direct and appoint, and shall and may hold such other meetings as the president of the said Society shall think necessary to call, or one of the vice-presidents of the said Society, at the request of any six members thereof shall call, of which special meetings notice shall be given in two of the public newspapers printed in the city of Philadelphia, at least two days before the time of meeting; at any of which quarterly or special meetings, or adjournments thereof, it shall and may be lawful for the said Society, or so many of them as shall meet, by a majority of voices to agree, to ordain and to establish such by-laws, rules, orders, and regulations as they shall judge necessary, for the well-ordering and governing the said Society; and for the well managing the affairs thereof, and to appoint such and so many committees, consisting of such of their members as they shall think necessary, to superintend the different departments of duties already undertaken by the Society heretofore subsisting, or hereafter to be undertaken by the Society, hereby established, and to receive the reports of such committees, and take such order thereon, as to them shall seem proper; and to fix and ascertain the terms and conditions upon which new members shall be admitted in the said Society, and upon which former members may be removed, and to define and ascertain the duties of the several officers and committees of the said Society, and to enforce the same by such reasonable fines and forfeitures to be imposed on delinquents, as they shall think proper, and for want of obedience in any of the members, committees, or officers of the said Society, to remove and displace them, and others to appoint, and generally to agree to, ordain, and establish all such bye-laws, rules, orders and regulations, for the well governing of the said Society, for perpetuating a succession of its officers and performing the duties they have undertaken, or shall undertake as the said Society, at any of their said quarterly meetings or special meetings or adjournments thereof, shall by a majority of voices determine to be right and proper. *Provided always nevertheless,* That no real or personal estate above value of sixty dollars shall be disposed of, or the right and estate of the Society therein shall be lessened or altered, for the less, nor any bye-law, rule, order or regulation of the said Society enacted, repealed or altered, nor any sum of money appropriated to any new use not before agreed upon by any of the said meetings or committees to be appointed, unless the president or one of the vice-presidents, and at least twenty members shall be present at such meeting, and a majority of those present shall agree to the same.

And provided also, That all and every the bye-laws, rules, orders and regulations already enacted and made, or hereafter to be enacted and made by the said Society, be reasonable in themselves and not contradictory to the constitution and laws of this commonwealth.

Section 5. *And be it further enacted by the authority aforesaid.* That the constitution of the Pennsylvania Society for promoting the abolition of slavery, and for the relief of free negroes unlawfully held in bondage, as enlarged at a meeting of the said Society held at Philadelphia, the twenty-third day of April, in the year one thousand seven hundred and eighty-seven, and all rules, orders, regulations and proceedings made and had by the said Society in pursuance thereof, be and they are hereby declared to be in full force and binding upon the said Society, by this act, created and incorporated, until the same shall be repealed, altered and annulled at a quarterly or special meeting or adjournment thereof, to be held in pursuance of this act, as fully and effectually as if the same were to be originally adopted by the said Society, hereby incorporated and created at one of their said meetings,

Section 6. *And be it further enacted by the authority aforesaid,* That until the next election which shall be held by the said Society in pursuance of this act, the said Benjamin Franklin shall be the president thereof, the said James Pemberton and Jonathan Penrose shall be the vice-presidents thereof, the said Benjamin Rush and Caspar Wistar shall be the secretaries thereof, the said James Starr shall be the treasurer thereof, and William Lewis, Myers Fisher, William Rawle, and John D. Coxe shall be the counsellors thereof, and that all and every the committee and committees heretofore appointed by the said Society for promoting the abolition of slavery and for the relief of free negroes unlawfully held in bondage, shall be and continue to be the officers and committees of the Society hereby created and incorporated, and shall report to, and account with the same, in the same manner as they would have done to the former Society in case this act had not passed.

Section 7. *And be it enacted by the authority aforesaid,* That this act shall in all things be construed in the most favorable and liberal manner to and for the said Society, in order to effectuate the privileges hereby to them granted; and that no misnomer of the said corporation in any deed, will, testament, gift, grant, demise, or other instrument of contract, or conveyance shall vitiate or defeat the same, if the said corporation shall be sufficiently described to ascertain the intent of the party or parties to give, devise, bequeath, convey, or assure to, or contract with the said corporation hereby created by the name aforesaid. Nor shall any non-user of the said privileges hereby granted create any forfeiture of the same, but the same may be exercised by the said corporation, and notwithstanding their failure to meet at any of the times herein specified, to hold their annual elections, the officers elected at any of the said annual elections shall continue to hold and exercise their offices until others shall be duly elected to succeed them, at some future meeting of the said corporation.

Signed by order of the House,

RICHARD PETERS, Speaker.

Enacted into a Law at Philadelphia, on Tuesday, the eighth day of December, in the year of our Lord, one thousand seven hundred and eighty-nine.

PETER ZACHARY LLOYD,

Clerk of the General Assembly.

CONSTITUTION

OF THE

PENNSYLVANIA SOCIETY

FOR

Promoting the Abolition of Slavery, Etc.

As revised and adopted Ninth mo., (September) 29th, 1859.

———•—•—•———

It having pleased the Creator of the world to make of one flesh all the children of men—it becomes them to consult and promote each others' happiness, as members of the same family, however diversified they may be, by color, situation, religion or different states of society. It is more especially the duty of those persons who profess to maintain for themselves the rights of human nature, and who acknowledge the obligations of Christianity, to use such means as are in their power, to extend the blessings of freedom to every part of the human race: and in a more particular manner, to such of their fellow-creatures as are entitled to freedom by the laws and constitutions of any of the United States, and who, notwithstanding, are detained in bondage by fraud or violence. From a full conviction of the truth and obligation of these principles—from a desire to diffuse them, wherever the miseries and vices of slavery exist, and in humble confidence of the favor and support of the Father of Mankind, the subscribers have associated themselves under the title of the "Pennsylvania Society for promoting the Abolition of Slavery, and the Relief of Free Negroes unlawfully held in Bondage, and for improving the condition of the African Race."

For effecting these purposes, they have adopted the following constitution :

I. The officers of this Society shall consist of a president, two vice-presidents, two secretaries, a treasurer, a librarian and twelve counsellors, viz., four from the city of Philadelphia, and the remaining eight from such other places as the Society may from time to time determine. A board of education of thirteen, an acting committee of seven, and a committee on property, of three members, all of whom shall be chosen annually by ballot, on the last Fifth-day called Thursday, in the month called December.

II. The president, or in his absence one of the vice-presidents, shall preside in all the meetings, and subscribe all the public acts of the Society. The president, or in his absence, either of the vice-presidents, shall moreover have the power of calling a special meeting of the Society whenever he shall judge proper. A special meeting shall likewise be called at any time, when six members of the Society shall concur in requesting it.

III. The secretaries shall keep records of the proceedings of the Society, and shall correspond with such persons, and societies, as may be judged necessary to promote the views and objects of the institution.

IV. The Treasurer shall keep all the monies and securities belonging to the Society, and shall pay all orders signed by the president or one of the vice-presidents, and countersigned by one of the secretaries, and also such orders as are referred to in Articles VII. and VIII. which orders shall be his vouchers for his expenditures.

He shall have charge of the corporate seal, and affix the same when required by the Society. He shall report quarterly the balance in the treasury, to the credit of each account, and annually render a full statement of his receipts and expenditures. He shall, before entering upon his office, give a bond of not less than eight hundred dollars, for the faithful discharge of his duties.

V. The librarian shall have charge of and keep a catalogue of the books and papers of the corporation, and see that they are preserved from loss or damage. He shall keep a record of all papers or books loaned, requiring the same to be returned to the library within one month.

VI. The business of the counsellors shall be to explain the laws and constitutions of the States, which relate to the emancipation of slaves, and to urge their claims to freedom, before such persons or courts as are authorized to decide upon them.

VII. The board of education shall superintend the schools established by the Society, and shall have the management of the funds appropriated to educational purposes. They shall also consider, suggest and supervise measures for the improvement of the condition of the colored people, and from time to time prepare, and with the consent of the Society publish statistics and reports thereon.

Five members shall constitute a quorum to transact the general concerns of the board. All orders, drawn by their chairman, and attested by their secretary, shall be paid by the treasurer of the Society. They shall keep regular minutes of their proceedings, and produce them at every stated meeting of the Society.

VIII. The acting committee shall transact such business as shall occur in the recess of the Society, and report the same at each quarterly meeting. They shall have a right, with the concurrence of the president or one of the vice presidents, to draw upon the treasurer for such sums of money as shall be necessary to carry on the business of their appoint-

4

ment; and be authorized to employ a clerk to transcribe their minutes into a book provided for the purpose. Four of them shall be a quorum.

IX. The committee on property shall have supervision over the real estate of the Society, and direct all necessary repairs.

X. No person shall be admitted to membership who has not been proposed at a previous meeting of the Society, nor shall an election take place in less than one month after the time of his being proposed. The concurrence by ballot of two-thirds of the members present at a stated meeting shall be necessary for the admission of a member.

Foreigners, or persons who do not reside in the city of Philadelphia, may be elected corresponding members of the Society, without being subject to an annual payment, and shall be admitted to the meetings of the Society during their residence in the city.

XI. Every member upon his admission, shall subscribe the constitution of the Society, and contribute one dollar annually, towards defraying its contingent expenses: (Provided, that any member paying at one time the sum of thirty dollars or upwards, shall be exempt from all future annual contributions.) If he neglects to pay the same for more than two years, he shall, upon due notice being given him of his delinquency, cease to be a member.

XII. The Society shall meet on the last Fifth-day called Thursday, in the months called March, June, September and December, at such place as shall be agreed to by a majority of the Society.

XIII. No person holding a slave shall be admitted a member of this Society.

XIV. No by-law or alteration of this constitution shall be made, without being proposed at a previous meeting. All questions shall be decided, where there is a division, by a majority of votes. In those cases where the Society is equally divided, the presiding officer shall have a casting vote.

A LIST

Of those who have been elected Members of the Society since its organization.

Members who have held office in the Society are in small capitals, the highest office to which they attained being stated. (Del.) signifies that the party was a delegate to one or more of the Abolition Conventions held from 1794 to 1837.

Arthur Thomas, Phila., Pa., 4 mo. 14, 1775.
Seymour Hart, " "
JOHN BALDWIN, Pres't, Phila., Pa., 4 mo. 14, 1775.
Thomas Wishart, Phila., Pa., 4 mo. 14, 1775.
SAMUEL DAVIS, Treas'r, Phila., Pa., 4 mo. 14, 1775.
THOMAS HARRISON, Sec'y, (del.), Phila., Pa., 4 mo. 14, 1775.
John Browne, Phila., Pa., 4 mo. 14, 1775.
Joel Zane, " "
Thomas Hood, Esq., Phila., Pa., 4 mo. 14, 1775.
James Morgan, Phila, Pa., 4 mo. 14, 1775.
Richard Price, " 5 mo. 29, 1775.
JAMES STARR, Treas'r, Phila., Pa. 5 mo. 29, 1775.

Cadwallader Dickinson, Phila., Pa., 5 mo. 29, 1775.
Wm. Lippincott, Phila., Pa., 5 mo. 29, 1775.
Amos Wickersham, " "
Chas. Eddy, " 8 mo. 23, 1775.
Joseph Shotwell, Jr., Phila., Pa., afterwards of N. J., 8 mo. 23, 1775.
Wm. Coates, Phila., Pa., 8 mo. 23, 1775.
Matthew Henderson, Phila. Pa., 8 mo. 23, 1775.
John Hamilton, Phila., Pa., 8 mo. 23, 1775.
John Davis, " "
Joshua Comly, " "
Thomas Morgan, " "
John Bull, Esq., " "

Interregnum from 11th mo. 27, 1775, to 2d mo. 10th, 1784, when the Society reorganized.

John Thomas, Phila., Pa., 2 mo. 16, 1784.
John Field, " "
Benjamin Hornor, " "
SAMUEL RICHARDS, Pres't, Phila., Pa., 2 mo. 16, 1784.
Wm. Zane, Phila., Pa., 2 mo. 16, 1784.
Jonathan Shoemaker, Phila., Pa., 2 mo. 23, 1784.
JOHN EVANS, Treas'r, Phila., Pa., 2 mo. 23, 1784.
Lambert Wilmer, Phila., Pa., 2 mo. 23, 1784.
JOHN TODD, Sec'y " "
JAMES WHITEALL, Pres't, Phila., Pa., 2 mo. 23, 1784.
Isaac Gray, Phila., Pa., 3 mo. 1, 1784.
Joseph Russell, " "
Edward Brooks, " "
John Morton, " "
Townsend Speakman, Phila., Pa., 3 mo. 1, 1784.
Richard Humphreys, (tailor), Phila., Pa., 3 mo. 8, 1784.
Samuel Baker, Phila., Pa., 3 mo. 8, 1784.
Chas. Jervis, " "
Thomas Armat, " "
Israel Hallowell, " "
Richard Jones, " "

John Litle, Phila., Pa., 3 mo. 15, 1784.
John Warner, " "
Daniel Seidrick " "
Andrew Carson, " "
Thomas Bartow, " "
Thomas Palmer, " "
Robert Evans, " "
Benjamin Myers, " "
Clement Biddle, " "
Jehu Eldridge, " "
Robert Wood, " "
Israel Whelen, " "
THOMAS MEREDITH, Pres't, Phila., Pa., 3 mo. 15, 1784.
Joseph Moore, Phila., Pa., 3 mo., 15, 1784.
Nathan Sellers, " "
David Sellers, " "
Isaac Parrish, " "
Zachariah Jess, Sec'y Delaware Abolition Society, Phila., Pa., afterwards of Del., 3 mo. 15, 1784.
ROBERT COE, Recorder, Phila., Pa., 3 mo. 15, 1784.
Robert Towers, Phila., Pa., 3 mo. 15, 1784.
Jacob Baker, " "
Pattison Hartshorne, Phila., Pa., 3 mo. 15, 1784.

Dr. Benjamin Rush, Pres't, del. and Pres't Abolition Convention, Phila., Pa., 3 mo. 15, 1784.

Wm. Poyntell. Phila., Pa., 8 mo., 30, 1784.

Philip Price, Kingsessing, Phila. Co., 8 mo. 30, 1784.

John Hunt, Jr., Kingsessing, Phila. Co., 8 mo. 30, 1784.

Thomas Poultney, Phila., Pa., 8 mo. 30, 1784.

Robert Morris, (miller), Frankford, Pa., 8 mo. 30, 1784.

Norris Jones, Chester Co., Pa., 8 mo. 30, 1784.

Abraham Sharpless, Chester Co., Pa., 8 mo. 30, 1784.

Thomas Eddy, (del.), Phila., Pa., afterwards of N. Y., 8 mo. 30, 1784.

Charles Crawford, Phila., Pa., 8 mo. 30, 1784.

Isaac Lloyd, Darby, Pa., 11 mo. 29, 1784.

Evan Owen, Phila.,   "   "

Isaac Massey, Chester Co., Pa., 11 mo. 29, 1784.

John Tolbert, Chester Co., Pa., 11 mo. 29, 1784.

Chas. Dingee, Chester Co , Pa., 11 mo. 29, 1784.

Thomas Shoemaker, Phila., Pa., 11 mo. 29, 1784.

Thomas Savery, Phila , Pa., 11 mo. 29, 1784.

George Eddy,   "   "

Isaac Weaver, Jr.,   "   "

Joseph Budd,   "   "

James Lewis,   "   "

Caleb Attmore,   "   "

John Jacobs, (son of Israel), Montgomery Co., Pa., 2 mo. 28, 1785.

Jonathan Penrose, Pres't, Philada., Pa., 2 mo. 28, 1785.

Wm. Trimble, Jr., Chester Co., Pa., 2 mo. 28, 1785.

Thomas Shields, Phila., Pa., 2 mo. 28, 1785.

Francis Bailey,   "   "

Jeremiah Paul,   "   "

Amos Harmer,   "   "

Alex. Hale,   "   5 mo. 30, 1785.

Dr. Andrew Spence, Phila., Pa., 5 mo. 30, 1785.

Richard Riley, Marcus Hook, Pa., 8 mo. 29, 1785.

Joseph Clark, Phila., Pa., 8 mo. 29, 1785.

Dr. John Morris,   "   "

John Morrison,   "   "

Major Wm. Jackson, Phila., Pa., 11 mo. 28, 1785.

Zachariah Poulson, Jr., Phila., Pa., 11 mo. 28, 1785.

Wm. Graham, Phila., Pa., 2 mo. 27, 1786.

Thomas Parker, V. Pres't, (del.), Phila. Pa., 2 mo. 27, 1786.

Ellis Yarnall, Phila., Pa., 2 mo. 27, 1786.

Zebulon Potts, Esq , Montgomery Co., Pa., 2 mo. 27, 1786.

John Wistar, (del.), New Jersey, 5 mo. 29, 1786.

Thomas Wistar, V. Pres't, Phila., Pa., 5 mo. 29, 1786.

Nathan Boys, Phila., Pa., 5 mo. 29, 1786.

Chas. Brown,   "   "

Jacob Shoemaker, Jr., Phila., Pa., 5 mo. 29, 1786.

Wm. Linnard, Phila., Pa., 5 mo. 29, 1786.

Wm. Ashby,   "   "

Jonathan Pugh, French Creek, Chester Co., 5 mo. 29, 1786.

John Oldden, Phila., Pa., 5 mo. 29, 1786.

Burton Wallace,   "   "

Duncan Stewart,   "   " .

Jacob Trasel,   "   "

Wm. McIlhenney,   "   8 mo. 28, 1786.

Isaac Pearson,   "   "

Wm. West, Chester Co., Pa., 8 mo. 28, 1786.

John Bartram, Jr. Phila., Pa., 8 mo. 28, 1786.

Reece John, French Creek, Chester Co., 8 mo. 28, 1786.

John Letchworth, V. Pres't, Phila., Pa., 8 mo. 28, 1786.

Caleb Lownes, Phila., Pa., 8 mo. 28, 1786.

Tench Coxe, Sec'y, Phila., Pa., 11 mo. 27, 1786.

Col. Francis Johnston, Phila., Pa., 11 mo. 27, 1786.

Joseph Sharpless, Phila., Pa., 11 mo. 27, 1786.

Thomas Rogers,   "   "

Dr. Benj. Say, (del.)   "   "

Joseph Lownes,   "   "

James Read, Esq.,   "   2 mo. 26, 1787.

John D. Coxe, Esq.   "   "

John Hutchinson,   "   "

Chas. Williams,   "   "

Dr. John Story,   "   "

John Poultney,   "   "

Philip Price, Jr.,   "   "

Isaac Bonsall,   "   "

David Lownes,   "   "

Peter Woglom,   "   "

Caleb Johnson,   "   4 mo. 23, 1787.

James Pemberton, Pres't, Phila., Pa., 4 mo. 23, 1787.

Hilary Baker, Esq., Mayor of Phila., Phila., Pa., 4 mo. 23, 1787.

Jonathan Willis, Jr., Phila., Pa., 4 mo. 23, 1787.

Dr. Benj. Franklin, Pres't, Phila., Pa., 4 mo. 23, 1787.

Caspar W. Haines, Phila., Pa., 4 mo. 23, 1787.
Samuel Pancoast, F., Phila. Pa., 4 mo. 23, 1787.
Conrad Hanse, Phila., Pa., 4 mo. 23, 1787.
Joseph Anthony, " "
John Dowers, " "
Benj. Johnson, Lancaster, Pa., "
George Rutter, W., Phila., " "
James Trimble, " "
Sharp Delany, " "
Dr. John Luther, Chester Co., Pa., 4 mo. 23, 1787.
Wm. Wronse, Phila., Pa., 4 mo. 23, 1787.
Wm. Temple Franklin, Phila., Pa., 4 mo. 23, 1787.
Dr. Casp. Wistar, Jr., Pres't, (del.), Phila., Pa., 4 mo. 23, 1787.
John Kaighn, Phila., Pa., 4 mo. 23, 1787.
Dr. James Hutchinson, Phila., Pa., 4 mo. 23, 1787.
Philip Benezet, Phila., Pa., 4 mo 23, 1787.
Rev. John Andrews, D. D., Phila., Pa., 4 mo. 23, 1787.
Samuel Updegrove, York Co., Pa., 4 mo. 23, 1787.
Rev. Wm. Rogers, D. D., V. P., (del.), Philadelphia, Pa., 4 mo. 23, 1787.
John Claypoole, Phila., Pa., 4 mo. 23, 1787.
Richard Peters, Esq., Phila., Pa., 4 mo. 23, 1787.
John Smith, Lancaster, afterwards of Phila., 4 mo. 23, 1787.
Dr. John Foulke, Phila., Pa., 4 mo. 23, 1787.
John Todd, Jr., " "
Bartholomew Wistar, " "
Thomas Paine, " "
Wm. Richards, " "
Joseph James, Phila., afterwards of N. Y., 4 mo. 23, 1787.
Dr. John Chapman, Bucks Co., Pa., 4 mo. 23, 1787.
Benj. Wright, York, Pa., 4 mo. 23, 1787.
James Smith, Jr., Esq., Phila., Pa., 4 mo. 23, 1787.
Wm. Rawle, Esq., Pres't, (del. and Pres't Abolition Con., Phila., Pa., 4 mo. 23, 1787.
James Phillips, England, 6 mo. 5, 1787.
David Barclay, " "
Capel Loft, " "
Thomas Day, London, "
Hon. John Jay, New York, "
Col. Mathew Clarkson, Pres't New York Manumission Society, New York, 6 mo. 5. 1787.
Granville Sharp, Cor. Sec'y London Society, London, 6 mo. 5, 1787.

Richard Wells, Phila., Pa., 6 mo. 5. 1787
Robert Waln, " "
Robert Robinson, England, "
Wm. Hollick, " "
Joseph Bacon, Phila., Pa., "
Nathan Allen Smith, Phila., Pa., "
Wm. Gibbons, Lancaster Co., Pa., "
Wm. Shaw, Philadelphia, " "
George Latimer, " " "
Joseph Crukshank, " " "
Samuel Emlen, Jr., " " "
Benj. Shoemaker, " " "
Samuel Coates, (del.), Phila., " "
George Fox, " " "
John W. Kittera, Lancaster, " "
John McCree, Sec'y, (Sec'y Abolition Convention), Phila., Pa., 6 mo. 5, 1787.
Bernard Fearis, " "
Thomas Lloyd, " "
George Aston, " "
John Hopkins, " "
James Jess, New Jersey, "
Dr. Richard Price, England, "
Dr. Thomas Clarkson, London, 6 mo. 5, 1787.
L'Abbé Raynal, France, 6 mo. 5, 1787.
Woolman Hickson, Maryland, 9 mo. 18, 1787.
Wm. Brisband, Lancaster Co., Pa., 9 mo. 18, 1787.
George Davis, Phila., Pa., 9 mo. 18, 1787.
Robert Taggart, " "
Jesse Waterman, " "
James Trinchard, " "
Joseph Gibbons, " "
Dr. Samuel Powell Griffits, V. Pres't, (del.), Phila., Pa., 9 mo. 18, 1787.
Wm. Honeyman, Phila., Pa., 9 mo. 18, 1787.
George Richie, " " "
David Cooper, New Jersey, "
Samuel Allison, " "
Thomas Stokes, " "
Andrew Geyer, Phila., Pa., "
Joseph Parker Norris, Sec'y, Phila., Pa., 1 mo. 2, 1788.
Samuel M. Fox, Phila., Pa., 1 mo. 2, 1788.
Clement Hall, (del.), Salem, N. J., "
Dr. Ebenezer Howell, Salem, N. J., 1 mo. 2, 1788.
Thomas Annesley, Phila., Pa., 1 mo. 2, 1788.
Abram Liddon, " "
Stephen Maxfield, " "
Joseph Williamson, Chester River, Md., 1 mo 2, 1788.
Thos. Richardson, New Garden, Md., 1 mo. 2, 1788.
Ebenezer Maule, Gunpowder, Md., 1 mo. 2, 1788.

Robert Veree, Abington, Pa., 1 mo. 2. 1788.
Jacob Parke, Phila., Pa., 1 mo. 2, 1788.
Noah Webster, Jr., Sec'y Connecticut Society, Connecticut, 1 mo. 2, 1788.
Samuel Hopkins, Newport, R. I., 4 mo. 7, 1788.
Benjamin Foster, Newport, R. I., 4 mo. 7, 1788.
Enos Hitchcock, Providence, R. I., 4 mo. 7, 1788.
John Boggs, Welsh Tract, Del., 4 mo. 7, 1788.
George Roberts, Phila., Pa., 4 mo. 7, 1788.
Thomas Norton,   "   "
Thomas Lawrence,   "   "
John Sloan, (del.), Haddonfield, N. J., 4 mo. 7, 1788.
Wm. Dillwyn, London, 7 mo. 7, 1788.
Israel Pleasants, Phila., Pa., 7 mo. 7, 1788.
Thos. Fitzgerald,   "   10 mo. 6, 1788.
Le Marquis de La Fayette, France, 10 mo. 6, 1788.
Stacy Biddle, New Jersey, 10 mo. 6, 1788.
Richard Waln,   "   "
John Peter Brisot de Warville, France, 10 mo. 6, 1788.
John Needles, Maryland, 1 mo. 5, 1789.
Warner Mifflin, Pres't Delaware Society, (del.), Delaware, 1 mo. 5, 1789.
Aaron Hughes, New Jersey, 1 mo. 5, 1789.
Thomas Redman, (del.), Haddonfield, N .J., 1 mo. 5, 1789.
Wm. Chancellor, Phila., Pa., 1 mo. 5, 1789.
John Bleakley,   "   "
George Wilson,   "   "
Dr. Solomon Bush, "   "
Mordecai Churchman, Phila., Pa., 1 mo. 5, 1789.
Wm. Kidd, Phila., Pa., 1 mo. 5, 1789.
John Ely,   "   "
James Oldden, "   "
John Saunders, Alexandria, Va., 1 mo. 5, 1789.
John Tegal, Virginia, 1 mo. 5, 1789.
George Corbyn, Virginia, 1 mo. 5, 1789.
John Roberts, Lancaster, Pa., 1 mo. 5, 1789.
Wm. Webb,   .   "   ".
Benj. West. Providence, R. I.,   "
Alex. Addison, Esq., Sec'y Washington, Pa., Society, Washington, Pa., 1 mo. 5, 1789.
Moses Brown, Treas. R. I. Soc., Providence, R. I., 4 mo. 1, 1789.
Thos. Gain, Boston, Mass., 4 mo. 1, 1789.
Wm. Pitt, Esq., London,   "
Thomas Clements, Chairman Salem Co. Society, (del.), Haddonfield, N. J., 7 mo. 20, 1789.

Wm. Patten, Newport, R. I., 4 mo. 1, 1789.
Samuel Vinson, "   "   "
Thos. Robinson, "   "   "
Jonathan Easton, "   "   "
Jno. Coakley Lettsom, London, 4 mo. 1, 1789.
Daniel Trotter, Phila., Pa., 4 mo. 1, 1789.
Benj. Taylor,   "   "   "
James B Bonsall, near Darby, Pa., 4 mo. 1, 1789.
Thos. Proctor, Phila., Pa., 4 mo. 1, 1789.
Ebenezer Breed,   "   "
Nathan Field,   "   "
Jeremiah Parker, "   "
Jonathan Jones,   "   "
Thomas Forrest,   "   "
Charton de la Terriere, France, "
Francis Clery Dupont,   "   "
John Mears, Northumberland Co., Pa., 4 mo. 1, 1789.
John Brown, near Dover, Del., 4 mo. 1, 1789.
John Smilie, Esq., Fayette Co., Pa., 4 mo. 1, 1789.
Matthew Hale, Phila., Pa., 7 mo. 20, 1789.
Joseph Inskeep,   "   "
Thomas Clements, Chairman, Salem Co., Society, (del.), Haddonfield, N. J., 7 mo. 20, 1789.
Rev. Nic. Collin, D. D., V. Pres't, Phila., Pa., 12 mo. 8, 1789.
Richard Parker, Phila., Pa., 12 mo. 8, 1789.
John Starr,   "   "
Samuel Kingsley, "   "
Caleb Carmalt,   "   "
Kearney Wharton, "   "
Benj. W. Morris, "   "
Robert Roberts,   "   "
Thomas Penrose,   "   "
Zaccheus Collins, "   "
Henry Hale Graham, Phila., Pa., 12 mo. 8, 1789.
Anthony Felix Wuibert, Phila , Pa., 12 mo. 8, 1789.
Sam'l Redwood, Phila., Pa., 12 mo. 8, 1789.
Rees Cadwallader, Redstone, Pa., 12 mo. 8, 1789.
Samuel Jackson, Chester Co., Pa., 12 mo. 8, 1789.
Eli Lewis, Little York, Pa., 12 mo. 8, 1789.
Benjamin Wright, New Jersey,   "
Caleb Kirk, Delaware,   "
Zebulon Hollingsworth, Esq., Baltimore, Md., 12 mo , 8, 1789.
John Richardson, Maryland, 12 mo. 8, 1789.
John Feigle,   "   "
Benj. West, Massachusetts,   "
Joseph Wilkinson. (del.), Md.,   "
Robert Kammersly, York Co., Pa., 1 mo. 4, 1790.

Thos. Fisher, York Co., Pa., 1 mo. 4, 1790.
Wm. Nelson,   "   "   "
Peter Mondirf,   "   "   "
AmbroseUpdegraff,"   "   "   "
John Morris,   "   "   "
James Smith,   "   "   "
Chas. Lukens,   "   "   "
Isaiah Harr,   "   "   "
Wm. Welsh,   "   "   "
S. Barnett,   "   "   "
Andrew Johnson,   "   "   "
Daniel May,   "   "   "
Richard Hill Morris, Chester Co., Pa., 1 mo.
    4, 1790.
Thos. Githen, Haddonfield, N. J., 1 mo. 4,
    1790.
Hezekiah Hughes, Salem, N. J., 1 mo. 4,
    1790.
Thos. Ross, West Chester, Pa., 1 mo. 4,
    1790.
John Stapler, Jr., Bucks Co., Pa., 1 mo. 4,
    1790.
Joseph Thomas, Phila., Pa., 1 mo. 4, 1790.
Samuel Claphamson,   "   "
Dr. Amos Gregg,   "   "
Girard Vogels,   "   "
Isaac Buckbee,   "   "
Joshua Gilpin,   "   "
Alexander Symington, "   4 mo. 5, 1790.
Thomas Ames,   "   "
John Brown, Jr.,   "   "
Wm. Delany,   "   "
Seth Willis,   "   "
Chas Evans,   "   "
Jesse Maris,   "   "
Geo. Roberts, F.,   "   "
Chas. Robertson,   "   "
Wm. Waring,   "   "
Jos. Cooper, Jr., New Jersey,   "
John Pope, Mansfield, N. J.,   "
John Denn, Salem,   "
Matthias Holstein, Darby, Pa., "
Nathaniel Newlin,   "   "
Joseph Hoskins, Chester Co., Pa.,   "
Joseph Sansom, Sec'y, Phila., Pa., 7 mo. 5,
    1790.
George Meade, Phila., Pa., 7 mo. 5, 1790.
George Williams, (del.), Phila., Pa., 7 mo.
    5, 1790.
Samuel Davis, Jr., Phila., Pa., 7 mo. 5,
    1790.
John Bringhurst, Phila., Pa., 7 mo. 5, 1790.
John Inskeep,   "   "
James Logan,   "   "
Joseph Waln,   "   "
Gideon Hill Wells,   "   "
James Jobson,   "   "
Thomas Hartley, York, Pa.,   "

Thomas Scott, Pres't Washington, Pa., Ab.
    Society, (del.), Washington, Pa., 7 mo.
    5, 1790.
Col. Absalom Baird, Treas'r Washington,
    Pa., Ab. Society, (del.), Washington,
    Pa., 7 mo. 5, 1790.
David Reddick, Vice Pres't Washington,
    Pa., Abolition Society, Washington, Pa.,
    7 mo. 5, 1790.
James Allison, Phila., Pa., 7 mo. 5, 1790.
Alexander Wright, "   "
William Graham, Chester, Pa.,   "
James McIlvain,   "   "
Robert Smith,   "   "
Dr. George Logan, Germantown, Pa, 7 mo.
    5, 1790.
John Vining, Delaware, 7 mo. 5, 1790.
Hon. Wm. Pinckney, Md., 7 mo. 5, 1790.
Philip Rodgers, Pres't Md. Society, Balti-
    more, Md., 7 mo. 5, 1790.
Joseph Townsend, Sec'y Maryland Society.
    (del.), Baltimore, Md., 7 mo. 5, 1790.
John Browne,   "   "
Elias Ellicott,   "   "
Jesse Hollingsworth, (del.), Baltimore, Md.,
    7 mo. 5, 1790.
Dr. Sparman, Stockholm, Sweden, 7 mo. 5,
    1790.
M. Vadstrom, Stockholm, Sweden, 7 mo. 5,
    1790.
Rev. Wm. White, D. D., Phila., Pa., 10 mo.
    4, 1790.
Joseph Shoemaker, Jr. Phila., Pa., 10 mo. 4,
    1790.
Samuel Sitgreaves, Easton, Pa., 10 mo. 4,
    1790.
Hon. Elias Boudinot, N. J., 10 mo. 4, 1790.
Robert Brown,   "   "
John Gaunt,   "   "
Thos. Ballanger,   "   "
Isaac Collins, Trenton, N. J.,   "
Hon. Joseph Bloomfield, Pres't New Jersey
    Society, (del. and Pres't Ab. Conven-
    tion), Burlington, New Jersey, 10 mo. 4,
    1790.
Dr. Lawrence, Burlington, N. J., 10 mo. 4,
    1790.
Theodore Sedgwick, Mass., 10 mo 4, 1790.
Samuel Neale, Cork, Ireland,   "
Samuel Hoare, Jr., London,   "
Wm. Wilberforce, England,   "
Dr. Erskine, Edinburg,   "
Dr. Samuel Stillman, Boston, Mass., 1 mo.
    3, 1791.
David Howell, Pres't R. I. Society, Pro-
    vidence, R. I., 1 mo. 3, 1791.
John Dorrance, V. Pres't R. I. Society, Pro-
    vidence, R. I., 1 mo. 3, 1791.

Thos. Arnold, Sec'y R. I. Society, Providence, R. I., 1 mo. 3, 1791.
Daniel Lyman, Providence, R. I., 1 mo. 3, 1791.
Geo. Benson, Providence, R. I., 1 mo. 3, 1791.
Wm. Patterson, New Jersey, 1 mo. 3, 1791.
Burgess Allison, " "
Henry Clifton, " "
Uriah Woolman, " "
Dr. Palmer, Augusta, Ga., 1 mo. 3, 1791.
Isaac Briggs, " "
Rev. Ezra Stiles, D. D., Pres't Conn. Society, Connecticut, 1 mo. 3. 1791.
David Austin, 2d Pres't Conn. Soc., Conn., 1 mo. 3, 1791.
Simeon Baldwin, Sec'y Conn. Soc., Conn., 1 mo. 3, 1791.
Timothy Jones, Treas'r Conn. Soc., Conn., 1 mo. 3, 1791.
Elizur Goodrich, Connecticut, 1 mo. 3, 1791.
Mark Leavenworth, " "
Capt. Wm. Lyons, " "
Dr. Ebenezer Beardsley," "
Dr, Jared Potter, " "
Stacy Potts, Harrisburg, Pa., "
Wm. Lucas, Phila., Pa., "
Joseph Few, " 4 mo. 4, 1791.
Rev. Jos. Pilmore, D. D., Phila., Pa., 4 mo. 4, 1791.
Israel Taylor, Phila., Pa., 4 mo. 4, 1791.
James Antrim, " "
Wm. Brown, Jr., " "
James Wilson, " "
Wm. Wyatt Fentham, Maryland, "
Jeremiah Smith, Phila., Pa., "
HON. WM. BINGHAM, Vice Pres't, Phila., Pa., 7 mo. 4, 1791.
John Trump, Philad'a., Pa., 7 mo. 4, 1791.
Thomas Paul, " "
Timothy Matlack, " "
Wm. Master, " "
Ebenezer Large, " "
Dr. Geo. Glentworth," "
Richard Hopkins, " "
Peter Stephen Duponceau, Esq., Phila., Pa., 7 mo 4, 1791.
Jesse Trump, Whitemarsh, 7 mo. 4, 1791.
Thos. W. Pryor, " "
Ephraim Steele, Carlisle, Pa., "
John Jordan, " "
Michael Hubley, Lancaster, Pa., "
John Patrick, Cumberland Co., Pa., 7 mo. 4, 1791.
Joshua Pusey, Jr., Chester Co., Pa., 7 mo. 4, 1791.
Richard Hartshorne, Pres't N. J., Society, del. and Pres't Ab. Con., New Jersey, 7 mo. 4, 1791.

Dr. Moses Bartram, South Carolina, 7 mo. 4, 1791.
Isaac Milnor, Phila., Pa., 4 mo. 2, 1792.
Casper W. Morris, " "
Robert Dawson, " "
Lewis Walker, " "
Samuel Foudray, " "
Wm. Wood, " "
George Steinmetz, " "
George S. Moore, " "
Samuel Sterrett, (del.), Baltimore, Md., 4 mo. 2, 1792.
Thomas Dixon, Baltimore, Md., 4 mo. 2, 1792.
George Churchman, Cecil Co., Md., 4 mo. 2, 1792.
Joseph Churchman, Cecil Co., Md., 4 mo. 2, 1792.
Richard Gardner, Phila., Pa., 7 mo. 2, 1792.
JAMES TODD, Sec., (del.), Phila., Pa., 7 mo. 2, 1792.
James Poultney, Phila., Pa., 7 mo. 2, 1792.
John Elmslie, Jr. " "
Dr. Daniel De Benneville, Phila., Pa., 7 mo. 2, 1792.
James Morris, Montgomery Co., Pa., 7 mo. 2, 1792.
John Shoemaker, Jr., Abington, 7 mo. 2, 1792.
Jonathan Shoemaker, Abington, 7 mo. 2, 1792.
Samuel Riddle, York, Pa., 7 mo. 2, 1792.
John Lukens, " "
Emmor Baily, Chester Co., Pa., "
Moses Marshall, " "
David Shields, Maryland, "
Morris Darling, " "
Wm. Brown, " "
Martin Eichelberger," "
John Keller, " "
Wm. Woods, " "
John Mitchell, " "
John Shultz, " "
John Mickle, " "
Abel Janney, Culpepper, Va., "
John Smith, Jr., York, Pa., 12 mo. 24, 1792.
Daniel Longstreth, Bucks Co., Pa., 12 mo. 24, 1792.
Jonathan Pickering, Bucks Co., Pa., 12 mo. 24, 1792.
Randall Malin, Jr., Chester Co., Pa., 12 mo. 24, 1792.
Joseph Malin, Chester Co., Pa., 12 mo. 24, 1792.
BENJAMIN KITE, Sec'y, Phila., Pa., 12 mo. 24, 1792.
James Winchester, (del.), Maryland, 12 mo. 24, 1792.

Joseph Price, Phila., Pa., 12 mo. 24, 1792.
Chas. James Fox, Esq., London, 12 mo. 24, 1792.
Joseph Barger, Phila., Pa., 4 mo. 1, 1793.
William Garrett, " "
Cornelius Barnes, " "
James Hardie, " "
Sallows Shewell, " "
John Hallowell, Esq.," "
Thomas Bartow, " "
ROBERT PATTERSON, V. Presid't. (del.), Phila., Pa., 4 mo. 1, 1793.
Benj. R. Morgan, (del.), Phila., Pa., 4 mo. 1, 1793.
Robert Hare, Philad'a, Pa., 4 mo. 1, 1793.
Owen Biddle, " "
Jonathan Carmalt, Jr., Phila., Pa., 4 mo. 1, 1793.
Jacob R. Howell, Phila., Pa., 4 mo. 1, 1793.
Peter Le Barbier Duplessis, Phila., Pa., 4 mo. 1, 1793.
John Malin, Chester Co., Pa., 4 mo. 1, 1793.
Charles Dilworth, Chester Co., Pa., 4 mo. 1, 1793.
John Talbot, Delaware Co., Pa., 4 mo. 1, 1793.
Seneca Lukens, Montgomery Co., Pa., 4 mo. 1, 1793.
Thomas Kennedy, Cumberland Co., Pa., 4 mo. 1, 1793.
Albertin Gallatin, Fayette Co., Pa., 4 mo. 1, 1793.
Abraham Inskeep, New Jersey, 4 mo. 1, 1793.
John Vanderwerf, Amsterdam, Holland, 4 mo. 1, 1793.
John Vanderwerf, Jr., Amsterdam, Holland, 4 mo. 1, 1793.
Nicholas Simon Van Winter, Leyden, 4 mo. 1, 1793.
Travis Tucker, near Norfolk, Va., 6 mo. 24, 1793.
John Smith, Delaware, 6 mo. 24, 1793.
Nathan Harper, Frankford, Pa., 6 mo. 24, 1793.
Joseph Thomas, (Flour Factor), Phila., Pa., 6 mo. 24, 1793.
Samuel Williams, Jr., Phila., Pa., 6 mo. 24, 1793.
George Booth, Phila., Pa., 6 mo. 24, 1793.
Peter Barker, Jr., " "
Dr. John Porter, " "
Jonathan Worrill, " "
John Harrison, (son of Thomas,) Phila., Pa., 6 mo. 24, 1793.
Wm. Richards, Lynn, England, 1 mo. 6, 1794.
William Martin, Chester, Pa., 1 mo. 6, 1794.

John Beatson, Hull, England, 1 mo. 6, 1794.
Wm. Allum, New York, "
Wm. Fox, London, England, "
Abraham Booth, " "
James Dore, " "
Dr. John Rippon, " "
Abraham Chapman, Bucks Co., Pa , "
Nathan F. Shewell, " "
Seth Chapman, Montgomery Co., Pa., 1 mo. 6, 1794.
Slator Clay, Montgomery Co., Pa., 1 mo. 6, 1794.
Dr. Joseph Pierce, Chester Co., Pa., 1 11 o. 6, 1794.
James Trevor, Burlington, N. J., 1 mo. 6, 1794.
WALTER FRANKLIN, Sec'y., (del.), and Pres't Ab. Conv., Phila., Pa, 1 mo 6, 1794.
John Coyle, " "
William Wigglesworth, Phila., Pa., 1 mo. 6, 1794.
John Nancarrow, Phila., Pa., 1 mo. 6, 1794.
Charles Shoemaker, " "
Thomas Dunn, " "
James Swain, N. Liberties, Phila. Co , 1 mo. 6, 1794.
Edward Farris, Phila., Pa., 1 mo. 6, 1794.
John Rively, Kingsessing, Phila. Co., 4 mo. 1, 1794.
William Preston, (Bricklayer), Phila., Pa., 4 mo. 1, 1794.
Joseph D. Drinker, (Merchant), Phila., Pa., 4 mo. 1, 1794.
Joseph Bedham Smith, Phila., Pa., 4 mo. 1, 1794.
TIMOTHY PAXSON, Sec'y, (del. and Pres't of Ab. Conv.), Phila., Pa., 7 mo. 3. 1794.
Thos. P. Cope, (del. and Treas'r Ab. Conv.), 7 mo. 3, 1794.
Solomon White, Phila., Pa., 7 mo. 3, 1794.
Edward Garrigues, " "
Thomas Say Bartram, " "
Daniel Dawson, " "
James Bringhurst. " "
Joseph Turner, Phila. Co., Pa., "
Wm. Gazzam, " "
Wm. Turner, " "
Wm. Barber, York, Pa., "
Watson Atkinson, Phila. Co., Pa., "
Benjamin Davis, Radnor. "
Thomas Wickersham, Talbot Co., Md., 7 mo. 3, 1794.
Chas. B. Brown, Phila., Pa., 9 mo. 23. 1794.
Israel Paxson, " "
BENJ. TUCKER, V. Pres't, (del.), Phila., Pa., 9 mo. 23, 1794.
Thomas Keel, Baltimore, 9 mo. 23, 1794.

Samuel Bettle, (del.), Phila., 9 mo., 23, 1794.
Daniel Thomas, Phila., Pa., 9 mo. 23, 1794.
John Poor,   "   "
James Little,   "   "
Ezekiel King,   "   "
Joseph Keen,   "   "
Leonard Sayre,   "   "
John McLeod,   "   "
Philip Jones, Jr.,   "   "
Thomas Jones,   "   "
John Jones,   "   "
Thos. Ustick, Phila. Co., Pa.,   "
Richard Hillier, Long Island,   "
Rev. Elhanan Winchester, London, "
Thos. Memminger, Bucks Co., Pa., "
Casper Wistar, Chester Co., Pa.,   "
Isaac Taylor,   "   "
Richard Strode,   "   "
Edward Darlington,   "   "
Cheyney Jefferies,   "   "
Benjamin Webber Oakford, Delaware Co.,
     Pa , 9 mo. 23. 1794.
Abr'm Shoemaker, Phila., Pa., 12 mo. 24, 1794
Robert Shewell, Phila., Pa., 12 mo. 24. 1794.
John Woodsides,   "   "
George S. Johannot, (del.), Baltimore, 12
     mo. 24, 1794.
Wm. Mott, Phila., Pa., 12 mo. 24, 1794.
Edward Stammer, "   "
John Stanford, New York,   "
Wm. Button, London,   "
Dr. John E. Harrison. England, "
Thomas Fleeson, Phila., Pa., 3 mo. 19, 1795.
Plunket F. Glentworth, "   "
Nathaniel Davis,   "   "
Thomas Randall,   "   "
Thomas Stewardson, "   "
John Hulme, Bucks Co., Pa.,   "
Robert Shewell,   "   "
Wm. Sharpless, Chester Co., Pa., 3 mo. 19.
Samuel Painter, Jr.,   "   "
Hugh Barclay, Bedford Co., Pa., "
Samuel Dexter, Massachusetts,   "
Morgan John Rhees, Wales,   "
Jonathan Gibbs, Phila., Pa., 7 mo. 3, 1795.
John Gardiner, Jr.,   "   "
Jared Mansfield,   "   "
Thomas W. Tallman, "   "
Abraham M. Garrigues, "   "
Thomas Carpenter,   "   "
Isaac Carlisle,   "   "
James Pilling,   "   "
John Vincent,   "   "
Edward Jones,   "   "
Wm. Taylor, Jr.,   "   "
David Kempton,   "   "
George Suckley,   "   "
Joshua R. Smith,   "   "

JAMES MILNOR, Sec'y, (del. and Pres't Ab.
     Conv.), Norristown, Pa., afterwards
     Phila., 9 mo. 25, 1795.
Joseph Gurney, London, 9 mo. 25, 1795.
John Gurney,   "   "
Robert Frazer, (del.), Chester Co., Pa., 9
     mo. 25. 1795.
Wm. Jones, (del.) Phila., Pa., 9 mo. 25,
     1795.
Jacob Johnson, Phila., Pa., 9 mo. 25, 1795.
Peter Smyth,   "   "
Wm. Young Birch, "   2 mo. 22, 1796.
Isaac T. Hopper, (del.), Phila., Pa., 2 mo.
     22, 1796.
John Derbyshire, Phila., Pa., 2 mo. 22, 1796.
John Ormrod,   "   "
Wm. Gibbons,   "   "
Emmor Kimber,   "   "
Wm. Smith, (Tailor), "   "
Elijah Waring,   "   "
Enoch Lewis,   "   "
George Ashbridge,   "   "
James Girvan,   "   "
Isaac Sermon,   "   "
Chas. Newbold,   "   "
Robert Pleasants,   "   "
Basil Wood,   "   "
Peter Helm,   "   "
John Griffiths,   "   "
Wm. Griffiths.   "   "
Joseph Hemphill, Chester Co., Pa., "
Isaac Bailey, Jr.,   "   "
Richard Barnard, Jr.,   "   "
Isaac Wilson,   "   "
John Jefferis,   "   "
Caleb Massey,   " 4 mo. 4, 1796.
Theophilus Foulke, Bucks Co., Pa., "
Joseph Taylor,   "   "
John Brown, Falls Township, Bucks Co.,
     4 mo. 4, 1796.
Thomas Lloyd, South Wales, 4 mo. 4, 1796.
Wm. Lownes, Falls Township, Bucks Co.,
     4 mo. 4, 1796.
John J. Parry, Phila., Pa., 6 mo. 28, 1796.
Wm. Barker,   "   "
Thos. Newnham,   "   "
Charlton Yeatman, "   "
Richard Mosley,   "   "
John Burk,   "   "
John Jones,   "   "
Jeffrey Smedley, Chester Co., Pa., "
John Fling, Phila., Pa., 10 mo. 3, 1796.
Gilbert Gaw, Jr., "   "
Titus Bennett,   "   "
W. Wright, Pres't Colum. Soc., (del.), Lan-
     caster Co., 10 mo. 3, 1796.
Othniel Alsop, (del. and Sec'y Abo. Conv.),
     Phila., Pa., 12 mo. 1, 1796.

Samuel Jones, Phila., Pa., 12 mo. 1, 1796.
Ezra Varden, "   "
Richard Lee, "   "
John Turner, "   "
Joseph Marshall, Jr.,"   "
Joseph Engle, "   "
John B. Ackley, "   "
Thomas Perkins, "   "
Matthew Watson, "   "
Samuel Wallis, Lycoming Co., Pa., 12 mo. 1, 1796.
John Adlum, Lycoming Co., Pa., 12 mo. 1, 1796.
Wm. Ellis, Lycoming Co., Pa., 12 mo. 1, 1796.
Caleb Hoopes, Chester Co., Pa., 12 mo. 1, 1796.
Thomas Taylor, Chester Co., Pa., 12 mo. 1, 1796.
James Lindley, Chester Co., Pa., 12 mo. 1, 1796.
Henry Hoopes, Chester Co., Pa., 12 mo. 1, 1796.
Robert Lambourn, Jr., Chester Co., Pa., 12 mo. 1, 1796.
Archibald McLean, Alexandria, Va., 12 mo. 1, 1796.
Samuel Garrigues, Jr., Phila., Pa., 2 mo. 14, 1797.
Joseph Dilworth, Phila., Pa., 2 mo. 14, 1797.
Gervas W. Johnson, "   "
Joseph Merrefield, "   "
Abraham Parker, "   "
Levi Garrett, "   "
Wm. A. Stokes, "   "
Henry Atherton, Jr., Bucks Co., Pa., "
Matthias Hutchinson, "   "
Wm. Buckman, "   "
Samuel Johnson, (Hatter),"   "
Samuel Brown, "   "
Joseph Roberts, Montgomery Township, Mont. Co., Pa., 2 mo. 14, 1797.
Benj. Evans, Wales, 2 mo. 14, 1797.
Wm. Nichols, Phila., Pa., 6 mo. 12, 1797.
Elisha Gordon, "   "
Matthew Carey, "   "
Samuel Shinn, "   "
Henry Holdship, "   "
Chas. Carey, "   "
Benj. Cresson "   "
James Strawbridge, "   "
Samuel Barnes, "   "
John D. Pinkerton, "   "
Henry Toland, "   "
Michael Keppele, Esq., Phila., Pa., 6 mo. 12, 1797.
Henry Drinker, Jr., Phila., Pa., 6 mo. 12, 1797.

Wm. Macbean, Phila., Pa., 6 mo. 12, 1797.
John Armstrong, "   "
Wm. Vicary, "   "
Wm. Penrose, Phila. Co., Pa., "
James Hopkins, Lancaster, Pa., "
Joshua Sullivan, Lower Dublin, "
Leger Feliceté Sonthonax, French Commissioner, Cape François, St. Domingo, 11 mo. 9, 1797.
Julien Raimond, French Commissioner, Cape François, St. Domingo, 11 mo. 9, 1797.
M. Pascal, Secretary General to French Commission, Cape François, St. Domingo, 11 mo. 9, 1797.
Benj. Giroud, Cape François, St. Domingo, 11 mo. 9, 1797.
Geo. Worrall, Phila., Pa., 11 mo. 9, 1797.
James Traquair, "   "
John Miller, M. C., "   "
John Lodor, "   "
Samuel Cooper, "   "
Edmund Kinsey, "   "
Daniel Smith, Northumberland Co., Pa., 11 mo. 9, 1797.
Thomas Vickers, Chester Co., Pa., 12 mo. 22, 1797.
Dr. Henry Yates Carter, Germantown, Pa., 12 mo. 22, 1797.
James Murray, Bucks Co., Pa., 12 mo. 22, 1797.
Ezekiel E. Maddock, Phila., Pa., 12 mo. 22, 1797.
Wm. L. Maddock, Phila., Pa., 12 mo. 22, 1797.
Ebenezer Hickling, Phila., Pa., 12 mo. 22, 1797.
Thomas Smith, (Printer), Phila., Pa., 5 mo. 28, 1798.
John J. Malcom, Phila., Pa., 5 mo. 28, 1798.
Richard Vidler, "   "
Samuel Lippincott, "   "
John Baily Wilson, "   "
Daniel Broadhead, Jr.,"   "
John Cadwallader, Huntingdon Co., Pa., 5 mo. 28, 1798.
Robert Patterson, Jr., Phila., Pa., 12 mo. 25, 1798.
Robert Cochran, Phila., Pa., 12 mo, 25, 1798.
Robert C. Martin, "   "
Oliver Evans, "   "
Richard Rush, Esq., Phila., Pa., 3 mo. 29, 1799.
James W. Clements. Phila., Pa., 3 mo. 29, 1799.
Joseph Reed, Esq., Phila., Pa., 3 mo. 29, 1799.
John Tiesworth, Northumberland Co., Pa., 3 mo. 29, 1799.

Joseph Sinton, Sunbury, Pa., 3 mo. 29, 1799.

George Taylor, Jr., Phila., Pa., 5 mo. 27, 1799.

SAMUEL HARVEY, Sec'y, Germantown, Pa., 5 mo. 27, 1799.

Samuel Smith, (currier), del., Phila., Pa., 5 mo. 27, 1799,

Joseph Hopkinson, (att'y), Phila., Pa., 5 mo. 27, 1799.

Wm. Griffith, Bedford Co., Pa., 5 mo. 27, 1799.

Thos. Peirce, Chester Co., Pa , 5 mo. 27, 1799.

Wm. Petrikin, Lycoming Co., Pa., 5 mo. 27, 1799.

Samuel Davis, Kent Co., Md. 5 mo. 27, 1799.

Philip Kinsey, Jr., Phila., Pa., 1 mo. 2, 1800.

Dr. Felix Pascalis,   "   "

John Reynell Coates, (del. and Sec'y Abo. Convention), Phila., Pa., 1 mo. 2, 1800.

Luke Cassin, Delaware Co., Pa., 1 mo. 2, 1800.

G. Washington Gibbons, Phila., Pa., 4 mo. 1, 1800.

Joshua Lippincott, Phila., Pa., 4 mo. 1. 1800.

Hanson Waters,   "   "

Nathaniel Chapman, Jr., Va.,   "

Abraham Hilyard, Phila., Pa., 9 mo. 29, 1800.

James A. Neal, Phila., Pa., 9 mo. 29, 1800.

Mordecai Wetherill,   "   "

Robert Taylor,   "   "

Solomon W. Conrad,   "   "

Richard Peters, Jr., (del. and Pres't Abo. Conv.), Phila., Pa., 9 mo. 29, 1800.

Chas. Townsend, Phila., Pa., 4 mo. 1, 1801.

JOHN BACON, Sec'y, (Sec'y Ab. Conv.), Phila., Pa., 4 mo. 1, 1801.

Abraham Lower, (del.), Phila., Pa., 4 mo. 1, 1801.

Chas. Allen, Phila., Pa., 4 mo. 1, 1801.

NATHAN SMITH, Sec'y, Phila., Pa., 4 mo. 1, 1801.

Thomas Stroud, Phila., Pa., 4 mo. 1, 1801.

Henry Baker,   "   "

James Tongue. Ann Arundell Co., Md., 4 mo. 1, 1801.

Josiah White, Phila., Pa., 7 mo. 4, 1801.

Joseph Wright, (sailmaker), Phila., Pa., 7 mo. 4. 1801.

Ephraim Haines, Phila., Pa., 7 mo. 4, 1801.

Samuel F. Bradford,   "   "

Joshua Longstreth,   "   "

Richard Wevill,   "   "

Joseph Trimble, Jr., Delaware Co., Pa , 7 mo. 4, 1801.

BENJ. WILLIAMS, (currier), Sec'y, (del. and Sec'y Abo, Conv.), Phila., Pa., 7 mo. 4, 1801.

John Meredith, Delaware Co., Pa., 7 mo. 4, 1801.

Matthew Llewellyn, Phila., Pa., 10 mo. 2, 1801.

Ebenezer Clark, Phila., Pa., 10 mo. 2, 1801.

John Dorsey,   "   "

Alexander Shaw,   "   "

John M. Smith,   "   "

George Vaux, (del.), "   12 mo. 31, 1801.

Jeremiah Warder, Jr.,"   "

Henry Dean,   "   "

Benj. Marshall,   "   7 mo. 1, 1802.

John Sergeant, (del. and Pres't Ab. Conv.), Philadelphia, Pa., 7 mo. 1, 1802.

James Robeson, Jr., Phila., Pa., 7 mo. 1, 1802.

Benj. Rowland, Montgomery Co., Pa., 7 mo. 1, 1802.

Thomas Marshall, Delaware Co., Pa., 7 mo. 1, 1802.

John Folwell, Phila., Pa., 3 mo. 1, 1803.

Caleb Wright,   "   "

JOSEPH M. PAUL, V. Pres't, (del.), Phila., Pa., 3 mo. 1, 1803.

John Partridge, (attorney), Elkton, Md., 3 mo. 1, 1803.

Dr. Wm. Shaw, Phila., Pa., 6 mo. 28, 1804.

John Brown, (silver plater), Phila., Pa., 6 mo. 28, 1808.

David McKinney, Phila., Pa., 6 mo. 28, 1804.

Lindsay Nicholson,   "   "

Archibald Binney,   "   "

James Ronaldson,   "   "

Thomas Bryan,   "   "

Samuel English,   "   "

Joseph R. Jenks, (del.), Phila., Pa., 9 mo. 29, 1804.

Evan Lewis, Jr., (del. and V. President Ab. Con.), Phila., Pa., 9 mo. 29, 1804.

Jacob S. Waln, Jr., (del. and Sec'y Ab. Conv.), 9 mo. 29, 1804.

Abel Satterthwaite, Phila., Pa., 9 mo. 29. 1804.

Benj. H. Smith, Delaware Co., Pa., 11 mo. 20, 1804.

Wm. Milnor, Bucks Co., Pa., 11 mo. 20, 1804.

John Kaighn, Phila., Pa., 11 mo. 20, 1804.

Thos. Owen, Jr.,   "   6 mo. 28, 1805.

Chas. Eberlee,   "   "

Job B. Remington, "   4 mo. 4, 1806.

Wm. Brown,   "   "

John Sims, (painter), Phila., Pa., 7 mo. 7, 1806.

Geo. D. Jones, Phila., Pa., 7 mo. 7, 1806.

JOSEPH PARKER. Sec'y, (del. and V. Pres't Ab. Con.), Phila., Pa., 7 mo. 7, 1806.

Joseph Ridgway, (tailor), Phila., Pa., 3 mo. 30, 1807.

Richard Pryor, (hatter), Phila., Pa., 3 mo. 30, 1807.

Thomas Kite, Phila., Pa., 6 mo. 22, 1807.
Wm. Delaney, Esq., "   "
Joseph D. Martin, "   "
ABRAHAM L. PENNOCK, Sec'y, (del. and Pres't Abolition Convention), Phila., Pa., 6 mo. 22, 1807.
Roberts Vaux, (del.), Phila., Pa., 6 mo. 22, 1807.
Chas. C. French, Phila., Pa., 6 mo. 6, 1807.
Nathan Dunn, "   "
Jesse Thomas, "   "
Thomas Field, "   "
Benj. Davis, "   " .
THOMAS PHIPPS, Tr'r," 12 mo. 21, 1807.
Joseph R. Hopkins, "   "
John Bradley, "   6 mo. 28, 1808.
Joseph T. Hallowell, "   "
John Parham, "   "
Benj. Mitchell, Jr., "   "
Matthew Semple, "   9 mo. 27, 1808.
Geo. Palmer, "   12 mo. 16, 1808.
Stephen Pike, (del.), " ,   "
Dr. William Price, "   3 mo. 31, 1809.
Jonah Thompson "   "
Joseph Walton "   11 mo. 8, 1809.
Isaac Smedley, "   9 mo. 4, 1810.
Jonathan Fell, Jr., "   4 mo. 3, 1812.
Israel Maule, "   "
David Jones, (hatter), "   "
WM. WAYNE, Jr., Pres't, (del.), Phila., Pa., 4 mo. 3, 1812.
Philip Price, Jr, (del.), Phila., Pa., 2 mo. 2, 1813.
Edward Parker, Phila., Pa., 2 mo. 2, 1813.
Wm. Milnor, "   3 mo. 15, 1813.
THOMAS SHIPLEY, Pres't, (del. and Pres't Ab. Con.), Phila., Pa., 3 mo. 15, 1813.
Chas. E. Smith, "   "
Joseph Lea, (del. and Treas'r Abol. Conv.), Phila., Pa., 3 mo. 15, 1813.
Asa Bassett, Phila., Pa., 12 mo. 8, 1813.
Wm. Bryant, "   "
Andrew Fisher, "   "
Ward Griffin, "   "
Wm. Carman, "   3 mo. 17, 1814.
Chas. Longstreth, "   "
Benj. H. Yarnall, "   "
Wm. Thomas, "   "
Dr. David J. Davis, Phila., Pa., 3 mo. 17, 1814.
Thomas Jacobs, Up. Providence, Montg'y Co., 3 mo. 17, 1814
John Barnett, Up. Providence, Montg'y Co., 3 mo. 17, 1814.
Samuel Webb, Phila., Pa., 3 mo. 30, 1815.
Benj. M. Hinchman, "   "
John Hinchman, "   "
EDWARD NEEDLES, Pres't, (del.), Phila., Pa., 3 mo. 25, 1816.

HENRY TROTH, Treas'r, Phila., Pa., 3 mo. 25, 1816.
John Elliott, Phila., Pa., 3 mo. 25, 1816.
Samuel Sellers, "   "
Wm. Folwell, Jr.," "   "
Benj. Albertson, "   "
Jacob F. Walter, "   "
JAMES MOTT, JR., Sec'y, (del.), Phila., Pa., 3 mo. 25, 1816.
John H. Willets, Phila., Pa., 3 mo. 25, 1816.
Powell Stackhouse, Phila., 9 mo. 23, 1816.
Jonathan Thomas, "   9 mo. 23, 1816.
George Bourne, "   "
Dr. Anthony Benezet, Phila., Pa. 12 mo. 19, 1816.
Benj. C. Parvin, (del.), Phila., Pa., 12 mo. 19, 1816.
Joseph McDowell, Phila., Pa., 12 mo. 19, 1816
DR. JOSEPH PARRISH, Pres't. (del.), Phila., Pa., 12 mo. 19, 1816.
Phillp Garrett, Phila., Pa., 12 mo. 19, 1816.
Wm. Kirkwood, Columbia, Pa., 12 mo. 19, 1816.
James Wright, Columbia, Pa., 12 mo. 19, 1816.
Jos. Mifflin, (del. and Sec. Columbia Abol. Society), Columbia, Pa., 12 mo. 19, 1816.
Caleb Richardson, (bookseller), Phila., Pa., 4 mo. 9, 1817.
Samuel Austin, (merchant), Phila., Pa. 4 mo. 9, 1817.
Wm. P. Paxson, Phila., Pa., 4 mo. 9, 1817.
Benj. C. White, "   "
Thomas P. May, Pottsgrove, Chester Co., Pa., 4 mo. 9, 1817.
Samuel Schaeffer, Coventry, Chester Co., Pa., 4 mo. 9, 1817.
Stephen Rossetter, Coventry, Chester Co., Pa., 4 mo. 9, 1817.
Mordecai Thomas, Coventry, Chester Co., Pa., 4 mo. 9, 1817.
Thos. Vickers, Chester Co., Pa., 6 mo. 20, 1817.
Wm. Harland, Phila., Pa., 6 mo. 20, 1817.
Wm. Kennard, Jr., "   "
Bartholomew Wistar, "   "
George A. Madeira, "   "
Joseph Askew, "   "
Samuel Griscom, "   "
Rev. George Boyd, (del.), N. L. Phila., Pa., 9 mo. 22, 1817.
Joseph Knight, Phila., Pa., 9 mo. 22, 1817.
Richard C. Wood, (del. and Sec'y Abolition Con.), Philadelphia, Pa., 9 mo. 22, 1817.
Joseph Rotch, "   "
Wm. Garrigues, Jr., "   "
Pleasants Winston, Richmond, Va., 9 mo. 22, 1817.
Thos Lewis, Chester Co., Pa., 9 mo. 22, 1817.

Dr. Wm. Staughton, Phila., Pa., 9 mo. 22, 1817.

DR. JONAS PRESTON, V. Pres't, (del. and Treas'r Abolition Conv.), Phila., Pa., 9 mo. 22, 1817.

Clement Laws, Phila., Pa., 9 mo. 22, 1817.

Luther Rice, Adams Co., Pa., 9 mo. 22, 1817.

David Worth, Phila., Pa., 9 mo. 22, 1817.

Ellis Stokes,   "   \   "

Thomas Christian, "   "

Joseph Pyle,   "   "

Samuel Smith, N. L. Phila., Pa., 9 mo. 22, 1817.

Nicholas Wireman, (son of Wm.), Adams Co., Pa., 9 mo. 22, 1817.

Jesse Russell, Adams Co., Pa., 9 mo. 22, 1817.

George Wilson,   "   "

Samuel Wright, (son of Benj.), Adams Co., 9 mo. 22, 1817.

Joseph Cloud, (U. S. Mint), Phila., Pa., 12 mo. 4, 1817.

Dr. Nathan Shoemaker, Phila., Pa., 12 mo. 4, 1817.

Joseph Cowperthwaite, Phila., Pa., 12 mo. 4, 1817.

BLAKEY SHARPLESS, Sec'y, Phila., Pa., 12 mo. 4. 1817.

Benj. M. Hollinshead, Phila., Pa., 12 mo. 4, 1817.

Joseph S. Kite, Phila., Pa., 12 mo. 4, 1817.

Richard Parker,   "   "

James R. Greaves,   "   "

Thomas Parker. Jr.,   "   "

Phineas Davis, York, Pa.,   "

Abner Thomas,   "   "

Augustus S. Kirk, "   "

David Paul Brown, (del.), Phila., Pa., 3 mo. 13, 1818.

Joseph M. Truman, Phila., Pa., 3 mo. 13, 1818.

John Field, Jr., Phila., Pa., 3 mo. 13. 1818.

Joseph G. Oliver, Milford, Del.,   "

Wm. P. Milnor, Phila., Pa., 6 mo. 1, 1818.

Adam Whann, Elkton, Md.,   "

Zebulon Rudulph,   "   "

Edward D. Corfield. Esq., N. L., Philada., Pa., 6 mo. 1, 1818.

Samuel C. Atkinson, Phila., Pa., 6 mo. 1, 1818.

Thomas Garrett, Jr., (del.), Darby, Pa., 6 mo. 1, 1818.

Wm. Davis, Phila., Pa., 6 mo. 1, 1818.

Ellis Yarnall, Jr.,   "   "

John Ella,   "   "

Joseph Roberts, Jr., Phila., Pa , 6 mo. 1, 1818.

John Bartlett,   "   "

Benj. Smith,   "   "

Ed. II. Bonsall,   "   "

James Wilson,   "   "

Moses Gillingham, Maryland, 6 mo. 1, 1818.

Thos. Gillingham,   "   "

Dr. Edwin A. Atlee, (del.), Phila , Pa., 6 mo. 1, 1818.

Townsend Sharpless, Phila, Pa., 6 mo. 1, 1818.

Jacob F. Wilkins, Phila., Pa., 6 mo. 1, 1818.

Lewis Wernwag, Phœnix Works, Chest. Co., 9 mo. 14, 1818.

George White, Phila., Pa., 9 mo. 14, 1818.

George Robinson,   "   "

George Peterson   "   "

Isaac Parry, N. L., Phila., Pa., 9 mo. 14, 1818.

David Weatherby, (del.), Phila., Pa., 9 mo. 14, 1818.

Daniel Smith, G., Phila, Pa., 9 mo. 14, 1818.

Dr. G. Burgin, Phila., Pa., 9 mo. 14, 1818.

Caleb Cresson,   "   "

Moses Lancaster, N. L., Phila., Pa., 9 mo. 14, 1818.

James Cox. Phila., Pa., 9 mo. 14, 1818.

Wm. Rawle, Jr., (del.), Phila , Pa., 9 mo. 14, 1818.

Jesse J. Maris, Delaware Co., Pa., 9 mo. 14, 1818.

John K. Garrett, Phila., Pa., 9 mo. 14, 1818.

Robert Murphey,   "   12 mo. 7, 1818.

Samuel B. Morris,   "   "

Solomon Temple, (del.), Phila., Pa., 12 mo. 7, 1818.

ISAAC BARTON, V. Pres't (del. & Treas'r Abolition Convention) Phila, 12 mo. 7, 1818,

Simon Wilmer, Swedesborough, N. J., 12 mo. 7, 1818.

Joseph E. McIlhenny, Phila., Pa., 3 mo. 22, 1819.

Thomas G. West, Phila., Pa., 3 mo. 22. 1819.

Geo. D. B. Keim, Reading, Pa., 3 mo. 22, 1819.

Wm. McIlhenny, Jr., Phila., Pa., 3 mo. 22, 1819.

A. Benezet Cleaveland, Phila., Pa., 3 mo. 22, 1819.

Wm. P. Richards, Phila., Pa., 3 mo. 22, 1819.

John Bechtel,   "   "

Joshua Wright,   "   "

Isaac Ellis, Montgomery Co.,   "

Wm. Kirk, Chester Co., Pa.,   "

David J. Snethan, N. L., Phila., Pa., 3 mo.

Benj. Stevens, Phila., Pa., 3 mo. 22, 1819.

James Givan,   "   "

Andrew Miller, Phila., Pa., 9 mo. 7, 1819.

John S. Pearson, near Reading, Pa., 9 mo. 7, 1819.

Hezekiah P. Sampson, Phila., 9 mo. 7, 1819.

Dr. Geo. S. Schott,   "   "

George Campbell,   "   "

Wm. A. Budd, Phila., 9 mo. 7, 1819.
Thomas J. Carlisle, "   "
James Hansell, "   "
George Widdifield, "   "
Caleb Carmalt, Jr., (del.), Phila., Pa., 9 mo. 7, 1819.
Curtis Taylor, Phila., Pa., 9 mo. 7, 1819.
Wm. Harris, "   "
John Antrim, "   "
James Rogers, "   "
Thomas Hale, "   "
Joseph H. Smith, "   "
Joseph Lukens, "   "
PETER WRIGHT, Treas'r, (del.), 9 mo. 7, 1819.
Richard B. Bowdle, Phila., Pa., 9 mo. 7, 1819.
Jacob T. Bunting, Phila., Pa., 9 mo. 7, 1819.
THOMAS RIDGWAY, Sec'y, (del.), Phila., Pa., 3 mo. 5, 1821.
John Wilson, Whitemarsh, Montgomery Co., Pa., 12 mo. 24, 1819.
Alan W. Corson, Whitemarsh, Montg'y Co., 12 mo. 24. 1819.
Isaac Jeanes, Whitemarsh, Montg'y Co., 12 mo. 24, 1819.
Wm. Jeanes, Whitemarsh, Montg'y Co., 12 mo. 24, 1819.
Samuel Felty, Whitemarsh, Montg'y Co., 12 mo. 24, 1819.
David Wilson, Whitemarsh, Montg'y Co., 12 mo. 24, 1819.
Samuel Malsby, Plymouth, Montg'y Co., 12 mo. 24, 1819.
John Henderson, Esq., Norristown, Pa., 12 mo. 24, 1819.
Joseph Thomas, Norristown, Pa., 11 mo. 24, 1819.
Dr. Isaac Huddleston, Norristown, Pa., 12 mo. 24, 1819.
Jacob Albertson, Plymouth, Montg'y Co., 12 mo. 24, 1819.
Dr. Joseph Leedom, Plymouth, Montg'y Co., 12 mo. 24, 1819.
Wm. Ellis, Norristown, Pa., 12 mo. 24, 1819.
Jonathan Ellis, "   "
Amos R. Ellis, White Plains, "
Hiram McNeil, Esq., Moreland, Montg'y Co., 12 mo. 24, 1819.
Justus Sheetz, Montgomery Co., Pa., 12 mo. 24, 1819.
Isaac Bellangee, Phila., Pa., 12 mo. 24, 1819.
SAMUEL MASON, Jr., Sec'y, Philadelphia, Pa., 12 mo. 24, 1819.
David Coggins, Phila., Pa., 12 mo. 24, 1819.
John Simmons, "   "
Isaac Jackson, Reading, Pa.,

John M. Ogden, Phila., Pa., 3 mo. 13, 1820.
Jonathan Conard, "   "
James W. Murray, (Att'y, del.) Phila., Pa., 3 mo. 13, 1820.
John Keating, Jr., (Att'y, del.), Phila., Pa., 3 mo. 13, 1820.
John Coles Lowber, (Att'y, del.), Phila., Pa., 3 mo. 13, 1820.
THOMAS EARLE, V. Pres't, (del.), Phila., Pa., 3 mo. 13, 1820.
Isaac Barker, Phila., Pa., 3 mo. 13, 1820.
Joshua Kimbel, " 6 mo. 5, 1820.
Peter Lehman, "   "
Samuel White, "   "
John B. Ellison, "   "
Robert Ellison, "   "
John Collard, Kensington, Phila., Pa., 6 mo. 5, 1820.
John B. Chapman, Northumberland Co., 6 mo. 5, 1820.
Dr. John M. Lynn, Phila., Pa., 9 mo. 26, 1820.
Gen. Wm. Duncan, Phila., Pa., 9 mo. 26, 1820.
Lewis Reese, Reading, Pa., 12 mo. 18, 1820.
Benj. Davis, "   "
Thomas Lewis, Robinson Township, Berks Co., 12 mo. 18, 1820.
Chas. Miner, West Chester, Pa., 12 mo. 18, 1820.
Wm. H. Dillingham, Esq , West Chester, Pa., 12 mo. 18, 1820.
John Paxson, Bensalem, Bucks Co., 12 mo. 18, 1820.
DANIEL NEALL, V. Pres't, Phila., Pa., 12 mo. 18, 1820.
Harman Yerkes, Jr., Whitemarsh, Pa., 12 mo. 18, 1820.
Joseph P. Norris, Jr., (del.), Phila., Pa., 3 mo. 5, 1821.
EDWARD B. GARRIGUES, Sec'y,(del.), Phila., Pa., 3 mo. 5, 1821.
Wm. Baker, (del.), Phila., Pa., 3 mo. 5, 1821.
Jesse W. Newport, (del.), Phila., Pa., 3 mo. 5, 1821.
John Livezey, Jr., Phila., Pa., 3 mo. 5, 1821.
Aquila Bolton, "   "
James Hutchinson, "   "
Aaron P. Wright, "   "
Wm. J. Brooks, W. Phila., Pa., 3 mo. 5, 1821.
Jason L. Fennimore, "   "
Thomas Penrose, "   "
George Getz, Reading, Pa., "
Walker Moore, Delaware, 6 mo. 18, 1821.
Joseph Phipps, Whitemarsh, Pa., 6 mo. 18, 1821.
Joseph Knight, Phila., Pa., 6 mo. 18, 1821

Joseph Evans, Phila., Pa., 6 mo. 18, 1821.
Henry Woodman, Tredeffin, "
Wm. R. Smith, Phila., Pa., "
Samuel Budd, " "
Hudson Middleton, " "
Samuel F. Moore, " "
Dr. Edwin P. Atlee, Sec'y, (del. and Sec'y of Abolition Convention, Phila., Pa., 12 mo. 3, 1821.
Isaac Elliott, " 12 mo. 3. 1821.
Joseph H. Smith, Phila., Pa., 12 mo. 3, 1821.
John Sarchett, " "
James Starr, Phila, Pa., 12 mo. 3, 1821.
Chas. W. Starr, Phila., Pa., 12 mo. 3, 1821.
Ebenezer Levick, " "
Jesse J. Spencer, Gwynned, Montg. Co., Pa., 12 mo. 3, 1821.
Evan Jones, Gwynned, Montg. Co., Pa., 12 mo. 3, 1821.
Chas. Jones, Norristown, Pa., 12 mo. 3, 1821.
Sam'l Edwards, Atty., Chester, Del. Co. Pa., 12 mo. 3, 1821.
Isaiah Hacker, Phila., Pa., 3 mo. 13, 1822.
David S. Brown, " "
Paul K. Hubbs, " "
John Jenkins, " "
Jos. W. Rowland, (del.) " "
Benj. Hanna, New Lisbon, O., 6 mo. 6, 1822.
Dr. Benj. Ellis, Phila., Pa., "
Alex. McDonald, " 3 mo. 4, 1821.
Isaac Lawrence, " "
Uriah Hunt, " "
Marshall Attmore, " 9 mo. 25, 1823.
Joseph Todhunter, " 12 mo. 25, 1823.
Wm. Brown, P., " 3 mo. 30, 1826.
David C. Wood. " "
Thos. A. Alexander, " "
Ellwood Walter, " "
Wm. J. Kirk, " "
Wm. S. Hallowell, " "
John Bouvier, Esq., (del.) Phila., Pa., 3 mo. 30, 1826.
Wm. Jones, Phila., Pa., 6 mo. 27, 1826.
Samuel Ross, " "
Isaac Williamson, " "
Robert Evans, " "
Edwin Walter, Sec'y, Phila, Pa., 6 mo. 27, 1826.
Chas. S. Cope, (del. and Sec'y of Abolition Con.), Phila., Pa., 6 mo. 27, 1826.
Jesse Stanley, Phila., Pa., 6 mo. 27, 1826.
Isaac Albertson, " 12 mo. 27, 1827.
Ezekiel Birdseye, Alabama, "
Jas. R. Wilson, Sc'y. Phila., Pa., "
Sam'l C. Sheppard, (del.) " "
Samuel Bispham, " "
Milton Smith, " 9 mo. 25, 1828.
Dr. Caleb Ash, " "

Enoch Lewis, Phila., Pa., 9 mo. 25, 1828.
Elliott Cresson, " "
Chas. Evans, (machinist), " "
Samuel C. Cooper, " "
James Rowland, Jr., " "
Thomas Booth, " "
James H. Lord, " 6 mo. 25, 1829.
Wm. Pritchett, " "
Chas. Alexander, " "
Joseph Sill, " "
Wm. Yates, " "
Dr. George Harris, " "
Samuel Clarke Atkinson, " 10 mo. 7, 1830.
Joshua C. Jenkins, " "
Joshua T. Jeanes, V. Pres't, Phila, Pa., 10 mo. 7, 1830.
Joseph R. Bolton, Phila., Pa., 10 mo. 7, 1830.
Dr. Geo. Burroughs, " "
Wm. L. Ward, Phila., Pa., 6 mo. 30, 1831.
John Paul, Jr., " 3 mo. 29, 1832.
Thomas Bowman, " "
Dr. Robert H. Rose, Silver Lake, Susq'na Co., 3 mo. 29, 1832.
Wm. S. Hansell, Phila., Pa., 6 mo. 12, 1832.
Thomas George, " "
Dr. Isaac Parrish, V. Pres't, Phila., Pa., 9 mo. 27, 1832.
George Sharswood, Esq., Phila., Pa., 9 mo. 27, 1832.
Benj. W. Bracken, Phila., Pa., 9 mo. 27, 1832.
Daniel Maule, Phila., Pa., 12 mo. 27, 1832.
Dillwyn Parrish, Pres't, (del.) Phila, Pa., 12 mo. 27, 1832.
Thomas Winn, Phila., Pa., 3 mo. 28, 1833.
George Griscom, Sec'y, Phila., Pa., 3 mo. 28, 1833.
Matthew Semple, Phila., Pa., 3 mo. 28, 1833.
Stacy Gauntt, " "
Dr. Fred Turnpenny, " "
Wm. A. Cochran, " "
Israel Corbit, " 9 mo. 26, 1833.
Chas. Gilpin, Phila, Pa., 9 mo. 26, 1833.
Wm. Henry, " "
Wm. Lloyd Garrison, Boston, Mass., 9 mo. 26, 1833.
Arnold Buffum, Boston, Mass. "
Benj. C. Bacon, Sec'y, Boston. Mass., afterwards Phila, Pa., 9 mo. 26, 1833.
John G. Whittier, Amesbury, Mass., 9 mo. 26, 1833.
Samuel J. May, Brooklyn, Conn., 9 mo. 26, 1833.
Simeon Jocelyn, New Haven, Mass., 9 mo. 26, 1833.
Arthur Tappan, New York, 9 mo. 26, 1833.
Chas. W. Dennison, " "
Benj. Lundy, (del.) Maryland, "
James Wood, Phila., Pa., 12 mo. 26, 1833.

Wm. Dorsey, Phila, Pa., 12 mo. 26, 1833.
CALEB CLOTHIER, Treas., Phila, 3 mo. 27, 1834.
Robert Alsop,   "   3 mo. 27, 1834.
Wm. J. Wainwright, "   9 mo 25, 1834.
Clayton Gaskill,   "   "
Wm. Whitman,   "   "
WM. C BETTS, Sec'y, "   "
Joseph Roberts, Jr.,   "   6 mo. 25, 1835.
Benj. S. Jones,   "   3 mo. 31, 1836.
CHAS. WISE, Libr'an, "   "
Chas. Evans,   "   "
Wm A. Garrigues, (del.) Phila., Pa., 3 mo. 31, 1836.
Chas. C. Jackson, Phila, Pa., 3 mo. 31, 1836.
George Pennock,   "   "
John Sharp, Jr.,   "   9 mo. 30, 1836.
George H Stuart,   "   "
EDWARD HOPPER, Sec'y, Phila, Pa.. 9 mo. 30, 1836.
LEWIS C. GUNN, Sec'y, Phila., Pa., (now of Cala.) 9 mo. 30, 1836.
WM. HARNED, V. Pres't, Phila., Pa., 9 mo. 30, 1836.
James M. Jackson, Phila., Pa., 9 mo. 30, 1836.
Wm. H. Scott, (del.) Phila., Pa., 9 mo. 30, 1836.
John Thomason, Phila., Pa., 9 mo. 30, 1836.
Abijah W. Thayer,   "   "
Edward M. Davis, Phila., Pa., 12 mo. 29, 1836.
Wm. Eyre,   "   12 mo. 29, 1836.
George Luther,   "   "
Rev. Henry Grew, Phila., Pa., 3 mo. 30, 1837.
David Knowles,   "   3 mo. 30, 1837.
John V. Wilson,   "   3 mo. 30, 1837.
Warner Justice, Phila., Pa., 3 mo. 30, 1837.
Wm. Sloanaker,   "   "
Sylvanus Root,   "   "
Gilbert S. Pryor, Phila, Pa., now of St. Louis, Mo., 3 mo. 30, 1837.
DR. JOSHUA RHOADS, Sec'y, Phila., Pa.. now of Jacksonville, Ill, 3 mo. 30, 1837.
Dan'l McLaughlin, Phila..Pa.,3 mo. 30, 1837.
George Alsop, Phila., Pa., 3 mo. 30, 1837.
Dr. Alfred Woodward, "   "
Wm. H. Ellis,   "   "
Wm. Johns,   "   "
Benj. J. Leedom,   "   "
John Longstreth,   "   "
Emlen Stackhouse,   "   "
John P. Crozier, Ashton Ridge, Del. Co., 3 mo. 30, 1837.
Wm. S. Lower, Phila., Pa., 3 mo. 30, 1837.
Martin Thayer, Phila., Pa., 3 mo. 30, 1837.
Joshua Mitchell,   "   1 mo. 26, 1838.
Wm. Lindsay,   "   3 mo. 29, 1838.
Chas. H. Thorne,   "   "
Eli Dillin, Phila., Pa., 3 mo. 28, 1838.

DANIEL NEALL, JR., Sec'y, Phila., Pa., 9 mo. 27, 1838.
Norwood Penrose,   "   4 mo. 11, 1839.
Richard Vaux,   "   "
Samuel C. Betts,   "   6 mo. 27, 1839.
Henry Cressman,   "   12 mo. 26, 1839.
John Houghton,   "   7 mo. 9, 1840.
Chas. C. Burleigh,   "   9 mo. 24, 1840.
Robert E. Evans,   "   12 mo. 31, 1840.
WM. D. PARRISH, Sec'y, Phila., Pa., 3 mo. 25, 1841.
Chas. D. Cleaveland, Phila., Pa., 6 mo. 30, 1842.
Simeon Collins, Phila., Pa., 6 mo. 30, 1842.
Elijah M. Neall,   "   6 mo. 30, 1842.
Stephen Byerly,   "   "
Wm. W. Cansler,   "   "
James Paul, Bucks Co., Pa.,   "
T ELLWOOD CHAPMAN, Vice-Prest., Phila., Pa., 6 mo. 30, 1842.
Thomas Hansell, Phila., Pa., 6 mo. 30, 1842.
David White,   "   "
John N. Ackley,   "   "
Amos Stackhouse,   "   "
Rollin H. Morgan,   "   "
JOSEPH LINDSAY, Sec'y, "   "
Samuel D. Hastings.   "   now of Wisconsin, 6 mo. 30, 1842.
Wm. Thompson, Phila., Pa., 6 mo. 30, 1842.
Robert Purvis,   "   "
BENJAMIN COATES, Vice-Prest., Phila., Pa., 6 mo. 30, 1842.
J. Miller McKim, Phila., Pa., 6 mo. 27, 1843.
John D. Griscom,   "   6 mo. 27, 1843.
HAWORTH WETHERALD, Sec'y, Phila., Pa., 6 mo. 27, 1843.
James P. Ellis, Phila., Pa., 12 mo. 28, 1843.
Hiram S Gilmore, Cincinnati, O., 12 mo. 28, 1843.
EDWARD LEWIS, Sec'y, Phila., Pa., 3 mo. 28, 1844.
Theodore L. Littlefield, Phila., Pa., 3 mo. 28, 1844.
Wm. C. Ivins, Phila., Pa., 3 mo. 28, 1844.
Wm. W. Moore,   "   "
Lewis Thompson, Phila., Pa., 7mo. 5, 1844.
Stephen E. Merrihew, Phila., Pa., 7 mo. 5, 1844.
Henry Kirk White Clarke, Phila. Pa., 7 mo. 5, 1844.
Henry Peterson, Phila., Pa., 7 mo. 5 1844.
Samuel Porter, Phila., Pa., 7 mo. 5, 1844.
Stacy Taylor,   "   12 mo. 26, 1844.
Rev. Lucius C. Matlack, Phila., Pa , 3 mo. 27, 1845.
Dr. Wm. Elder, Phila., Pa., 3 mo. 26. 1846.
Wm. B. Thomas, Phila., Pa., 6 mo. 25, 1846.
Jacob B. Shannon, Phila., Pa., 6 mo. 25, 1846.
Wm. J. Mullen, Phila., Pa., 6 mo. 25, 1846.

Truman B. Shew, Phila., Pa., 12mo. 31, 1846.
Robert Stackhouse, " "
PASSMORE WILLIAMSON, Sec'y, Phila., Pa.,
  3 mo. 25, 1847.
Wm. J. Canby, Phila., Pa., 6 mo. 24, 1847.
Daniel L. Miller, Jr., " 3 mo. 30, 1848.
George D. Parrish, " "
Samuel R. Shipley, " 6 mo. 29, 1848.
Edward Parrish, " 9 mo. 29, 1848.
Dr. Alfred L. Kennedy, Phila., Pa., 9 mo. 29,
  1848.
Ezekiel Jackson, " 3 mo. 29, 1849.
JOSEPH HEALEY, Sec'y," 6 mo. 27, 1850.
Samuel W. Townsend, Phila., Pa., 7 mo. 15,
  1852.
Dr. Wm. P. Tilden, California, 7 mo. 15, 1852.
Cyrus Whitson, Phila., Pa., 3 mo. 31, 1853.
John Sheddon, " 3 mo. 31, 1853.
JOSEPH M. TRUMAN, JR., Sec'y, Phila, Pa.,
  12 mo. 29, 1853.
Jonathan Roberts, Jr., Phila., Pa., 12 mo. 29,
  1853.
George W. Taylor, Phila., now of Chester Co.,
  Co., Pa., 12 mo. 29, 1853.
Samuel Parrish, Phila., Pa., 12 mo. 29, 1853.
Caleb H. Needles, " " "
Wm. Birney, " " "
George Orr, Phila., Pa., 3 mo. 30, 1854.
Pliny Earle Chase, Phila., Pa., 4 mo. 5, 1855.
Joshua L. Hallowell, Phila., Pa., 4 mo. 5,
  1855.
Llewellyn Truman, Phila., Pa., 4 mo. 2, 1856.
Augustus B. Shipley, Phila., Pa., 4 mo. 2, 1856.
Marmaduke C. Cope, Phila., 6 mo. 26, 1856.
Anthony M. Kimber, " " "
Francis H. Ray, New York, 3 mo. 26, 1857.
H. Ryland Warriner, Phila., Pa., 3 mo. 25,
  1858.
Spencer Roberts, Phila., Pa., 3 mo. 25, 1858.
Joseph Yardley, Phila., Pa., 9 mo. 30, 1858.
AMOS HILLBORN, Sec'y, Phila., Pa., 9 mo. 30,
  1858.
Reuben Tomlinson, Phila., Pa., now of South
  Carolina, 9 mo. 30, 1858.
Richard P. Hallowell, Boston, Mass, 9 mo.
  30, 1858.
Samuel S. Ash, Phila., Pa., 9 mo. 30, 1858.
Edward N. Hallowell, Phila., Pa., afterwards
  of Boston, Mass., 3 mo. 31, 1859.
Enoch Lewis. Jr., Phila., Pa., 3 mo. 31, 1859.
Thomas W. Braidwood, Phila., Pa., 6 mo. 30,
  1859.
Jas. M. Walton, Phila., Pa., 12 mo. 29, 1859.
Edward H. Steel, Phila., Pa., 12 mo. 29, 1859.
Harrison Dixon, Phila., Pa., 12 mo. 29, 1859.
WM. HEACOCK, Sec'y, " " "
LUKENS WEBSTER, Sec'y, Phila., Pa., 12 mo.
  29, 1859.

James G. Thompson, now of South Carolina,
  12 mo. 29, 1859.
Wm. W. Justice, now of S. Carolina, 12 mo.
  29, 1859.
Jonathan Roberts, Jr., " 12 mo. 29, 1853.
Wm. Birney, " "
George Orr, " 3 mo. 30, 1854.
Isaac H. Clothier, Phila., Pa., 6 mo. 28, 1860.
Dr. Jas. Truman, " "
Joseph Wood, " "
Chas. Sumner, Mass., "
Owen Lovejoy, Illinois, "
Rev. John G. Fee, Kentucky, "
Joshua R. Giddings, Ohio, "
Frederick Douglass, Washington, D. C., 6
  mo. 28, 1860.
George Thompson, England, 6 mo. 28, 1860.
Thos. M. Coleman, Phila., Pa., 9 mo. 25, 1862.
Augustus Simon, " "
Geo. E. Baker, Washington, D.C., 12 mo. 26,
  1862.
William M. Levick, Phila., Pa., "
Macpherson Saunders, " "
Wm. Forster Mitchell, Lynn, Mass., "
Geo. N. Hobensack, Phila. Pa., 6 mo. 25, 1863.
Marcellus Balderston, " "
Samuel E. Dickinson, " "
John Moore, " 9 mo. 24, 1863.
Wm. Folwell, " 3 mo. 31, 1864.
Alfred H. Love, " 6 mo. 30, 1864.
Joseph R. Rhoads, " "
Henry M. Laing, " 9 mo. 29, 1864.
Dr. Geo. Truman, " "
Oliver H. Wilson, " "
Joseph P. Cooper, " 3 mo. 30, 1865.
Mordecai Buzby, " 12 mo. 28, 1865.
Charles Lewars, " "
Peter K. Landis, " "
Hector McIntosh, " 3 mo. 29, 1866.
John W. Hurn, " "
Franklin S. Wilson, " "
Abraham W. Haines, " "
John C. Savery, " "
Samuel H. Gartley, " 9 mo. 27, 1866.
John A. Robinson, " "
William R. Chapman, " "
Dr. Wm. Savery, " "
Benjamin P. Hunt, " 12 mo. 27, 1866.
Edwin L. Dickinson, Wash., D.C., "
Henry C. Phillips, Phila., Pa., "
Samuel Conard, Phila., Pa., 3 mo. 28, 1867.
Robert R. Corson, " 12 mo 26, 1867.
William Still, " "
Octavius V. Catto, " "
Ebenezer D. Bassett, Phila., 12 mo. 26, 1867.
Jacob C. White, Jr., " "
Stephen Smith, " 3 mo. 26, 1868
William Whipper, " "

APPENDIX.

STATE HOUSE, BOSTON, March 29th, 1875.

My Dear friend Still:—I have just received your note of the 27th, with printed invitation of The Pennsylvania Society for Promoting the Abolition of Slavery, &c. &c., to attend the Centennial Anniversary of the Society, in Philadelphia, on the 14th of April next. I thank you, individually and as one of the Committee of Arrangements, for kind remembrance of me and for the honor done to me by your invitation.

How full of wonderful history is the Century now just closing; how dark with shame to vast numbers who once were deemed chiefs and leaders of the Nation in State and in Church; but how bright with honors and glorious triumphs to that grand old Society, in whose name and behalf you are now privileged to act! From the days of its infancy, when Benjamin Franklin was its first President and Dr. Rush was a membership in himself, down through the darkest days of Slavery's insolent domination and those of its ignominious downfall in the midst of treason and rebellion—and to the present hour, when its arduous, perilous, courageous labors have been spread over One Hundred Years, and it is entering into the reward of those labors,—it has deserved well of the Country and of Mankind; it has made for itself a most honorable record;—"the blessing of him who was ready to perish" has been continually upon it, in all its years; and it may well receive now, from every friend of our country, from every friend of a true and broad humanity, the greeting, "Well done, good and faithful servant!"

My work here forbids my accepting your invitation, which otherwise I would joyfully do. My heartiest good wishes are yours for a pleasant and absolutely successful occasion—when it shall seem to you all to be the blessed in-gathering of the harvest of the seed sown in such darkness and discouragement one hundred years ago.

With respect and affectionate regard. Your friend,

SAMUEL MAY.

———

WEST NEW BRIDGETON,
STATEN ISLAND, N. Y., March 25, 1875.

MR. WILLIAM STILL.

My Dear Sir:—I have your very kind note of the 20th, and the handsome copy of your book, for which I thank you sincerely. It is, as I see, a unique chapter of our history, and an almost indispensable supplement

5

to Mr. Wilson's History of the Slave Power, showing, as it does, the nature of that cruel wrong, and the heroism of its victims and their friends.

Your invitation to the Centennial meeting of the 14th of April, is very tempting, and I would most gladly join you and your associates in commemorating your good work. But I have been long engaged to be in Massachusetts on the 19th, and, with my other necessary duties, it would be impossible for me to be with you. But you will be sure of my hearty sympathy and God-speed, as in every word and deed for the elevation of every class of your countrymen.

With great regard, very faithfully yours,
GEORGE WILLIAM CURTIS.

KAOLIN, PA., 4th Mo. 12th, 1875.

WILLIAM STILL, Chairman, etc:

Dear friend:—Thy letter of invitation to the Centennial Anniversary of "The Pennsylvania Society for Promoting the Abolition of Slavery, etc.," signed by thee and by my friends, Dillwyn Parrish, Passmore Williamson, Joseph M. Truman, Jr., and Henry M. Laing, also; together with a copy of the programme and a ticket of admission to the platform, have been received. It will afford me pleasure thus to unite with my anti-slavery friends and coadjutors on that occasion.

Having in my minority, half a century ago, felt deeply the wrongs imposed on so large a portion of my fellow-creatures, so unjustly held in slavery, I then deemed it my duty to abstain as far as possible from the products obtained by slave labor; and it has ever since seemed to me to be a proper Christian testimony against that "sum of all villainies."

As thou and all the rest of the signers of the invitation, are well acquainted with my twenty years' effort in Philadelphia, to promote the free labor testimony, I need only to allude to it; if, indeed, a becoming modesty should not even preclude any reference to my connection with it at all.

It will afford me great pleasure to find present, in the capacity of chairman, the Hon. Henry Wilson, Vice President of the United States, whom I should gladly welcome as our next President of the U. S. It will be very pleasant also, to meet those who are expected to speak on the occasion. Very truly thy friend,

GEO. W. TAYLOR.

NEW YORK, 4th Mo. 9, 1875.

DILLWYN PARRISH, WILLIAM STILL, and others, Committee of Arrangements:

Dear friends:—I find, since acknowledging a few days ago, the receipt of your invitation, and expressing a purpose to attend your approaching Centennial Anniversary, on the 14th inst., that I shall be detained by duties here.

The anniversary which you commemorate, will have a peculiar and exceptional interest to all who shared in the labors of the anti-slavery conflict, and to all who realize the philanthropic need which still remains to aid those who were so lately enslaved, to surmount and conquer the disabilities by which they are still surrounded.

While rejoicing, as all may and should, with reverent thanksgiving over the great and beneficent work accomplished in the emancipation of four million of slaves, I trust the members and friends of your venerable and truly honorable society, will still continue its important and much-needed efforts for "improving the condition of the African race," until colored people are also emancipated from the yet prevalent, oppressive, cruel, and unchristian spirit of caste. Regretting that I shall not have the pleasure of meeting with you, a I had hoped,

I am cordially yours,   AARON M. POWELL.

---

311 EAST 62d STREET, NEW YORK, April 11, 1875.

My Dear Brother Still:—I have your letter forwarding to me the invitation of the Committee of the Centennial Anniversary of the Pennsylvania Society for Promoting the Abolition of Slavery, etc., to be present, and participate in said Centennial; for which, please accept for yourselt, and others of the Committee, my thanks. I should have made an earlier reply, had I not hoped to have been present with you, which would have been very gratifying; but finding that I could not be, it is due to you that I should acknowledge the receipt of your invitation.

Allow me to say that although a Decade has past since Chattel Slavery ceased to exist in our Country, and therefore the system, the Abolition of which was the prime object which led to the formation and continuance of your Society, yet I think it is commendable in the Managers thereof, that they have continued its existence to its Centennial year. No other former Philanthropic Voluntary Association connected with American History has lived to reach its Century; and it will be news to the American People that your Society is a year older than the American Nation, as it will that a Centennial ago your predecessors associated themselves to war against Slavery.

Although Slavery is gone, and its victims are recognized in law as American Citizens, and the equals of other American Citizens, yet the sad fruits of the system remain; in the memory, ignorance and moral turpitude which it fostered and entailed upon its victims; also in the cherished erroneous ideas of them, and the unchristian prejudice toward them; all of which to correct and eradicate, is the work of years; and which your Society, in its future, may well set itself to do; a work which involves as well, the happiness of the whole American People, as it does the higher manhood, and the progress and happiness of our brothers, the former victims of Slavery.

I hope Providence will give you Sunny Skies for the occasion, and that the interest therein, will bring together a goodly number of the veteran workers for the Abolition of Slavery, that was.

Respectfully and Truly,   CHARLES B. RAY.

DEDHAM, MASS., March 9, 1875.

My Dear Mr. Still:—I thank you very much for the kind invitation of the Pennsylvania Society for Promoting the Abolition of Slavery, etc., which you have had the goodness to forward to me. It would give me great pleasure to assist at the Centennial Anniversary of that Society, which has numbered so many excellent and illustrious men among its members, and which has led the way in the moral warfare which has resulted in the Abolition of Slavery. But I fear that it will be quite impossible for me to do so. I trust that your Celebration will be as successful as your warmest wishes could hope for. I am, my dear Mr. Still,

Very faithfully yours,

MR. WM. STILL.   EDMUND QUINCY.

————

BOSTON, APRIL 8TH, '75.

W. STILL and others of the Pennsylvania Society in behalf of the colored race. *Gentlemen and Brethren :*—

Owing to some little mishap,—a slight misnomer in the outward address of your note inviting my attendance and participation in your forthcoming "Centennial," of the 14th inst., I did not receive it till too late for such expression of my sympathy with the occasion as I would gladly have given you. I regret also, to say that I am, just now, too much of an invalid to bear the fatigue of even so pleasant a journey as that to which you invite me, with the prospect, too, of meeting such dear friends as Dr Furness, Garrison, Phillips, Douglass, and Whittier. But I can, at least assure you of my cordial sympathy with all the benevolent purposes you entertain towards the colored race, as enumerated in your circular.

It is every way fitting and right that thus in *"Philadelphia,"* the city of *Brotherly Love,* as its *name* imports, should centre and be manifest such largeness of philanthropy, and such breadth of charity! May God Almighty bless and prosper you therein.

With renewed expression of my regret at my being unable to visit you and participate in your celebration, and with repetition of my commendation of your purpose to keep alive benevolent action and service toward the colored population everywhere, I am your friend and co-laborer,

JOHN T. SARGENT.

————

MT. PLEASANT, IOWA, 4th Mo. 1, 1875.

To the Committee of Arrangements of the Penna. Abolition Society.

Dear Friends :—Your invitation to "attend and participate in the Centennial Anniversary" of your Society was duly received and the *honor highly* appreciated.

Much has been said about the *sacrifices* made in effecting the Emancipation of the slaves, and promoting the relief of those American citizens called Africans.

I rejoice in the feeling that I cannot remember when I was *converted* to this church of freedom.

It must have been *in the blood*, for from my first knowledge of the institution of the hateful system of slavery I loathed it as a vile curse on the earth.

Notwithstanding I have with many better men and women, been *anathematized* for participating in this movement, I feel *this day* with whitened beard, that I have made *no sacrifices*—but found it all the way through a compensating business, and I am *richer* for whatever I have said or done on behalf of the oppressed.

Though my tabernacle of flesh will be on the western side of the Mississippi, my spirit will leap over the prairies and mountains to mingle with, and breathe a benediction upon you, on the deeply interesting occasion of your centennial. I shall pray without ceasing that those who celebrate the next, may witness the entire extermination of slavery from the world, and the establishment of a code of peace among the nations that shall supercede forever the bloody scourge of war on the battle field.

With very kind consideration I am your cordial friend,

JOSEPH A. DUGDALE.

---

61 W. 17th Street, NEW YORK, April 10, 1874.

MY DEAR MR. STILL:

I find that I must forego the pleasure of attending the Centennial Anniversary of the Pennsylvania Abolition Society, to which you so cordially invite me. I very much regret to lose such an opportunity of greeting men and women, to whose faithful labors the country is so deeply indebted, for the extinction of American slavery, and for all the blessings that have followed that grand achievement. As your society was the earliest of all the anti-slavery associations formed in this country, so, also, I believe, is it the only one that survives the accomplishment of its main purpose, and remains in the field to assist in the education and development of the emancipated class. That its labors to this end may be abundantly blessed, and that your celebration may serve to deepen and intensify in the hearts of the American people, the love of universal liberty, is the desire and hope of

Yours, fraternally,   OLIVER JOHNSON.

---

103 W. SPRINGFIELD ST., BOSTON, April 8th, 1875.

My Dear Friend, Wm. Still:—I am very glad that our friends of the old "Pennsylvania Society for Promoting the Abolition of Slavery and for the Relief of Free Negroes unlawfully held in Bondage, and for Improving the condition of the African Race"—are going to commemorate the Centennial of its formation.

So quiet and Quaker-like have been the operations of the Society, that most of us, at this distance, hardly knew of its existence and history, nor of the amount of good it had been doing, in its silent, unobtrusive way, for so long a period.

I trust that the very competent Committee, who have the management of the meeting in hand, and especially the Historical Orator, Dr. Wm. Elder,—will furnish to the world, from the ample materials in their possession, a connected story of the doings of the Society,—culminating in the wider and better-known operations of the Anti-slavery movements of our own time.

I should enjoy very much the meeting of dear old friends of Reform on that occasion, but must deny myself that pleasure.

With kind remembrances of yourself and of your valuable work—the "Underground Railroad," I am Cordially Yours,

ROBERT F. WALLCUT.

———

IRVINGTON, IND., April 9, 1875.

DEAR MR. STILL:—

Your letter inviting me to attend the Centennial Anniversary of "The Pennsylvania Society for Promoting the Abolition of Slavery," on the 14th of the present month, was received a few days since. It would afford very great pleasure to be able to accept this invitation, but circumstances, I fear, will make it impracticable. I shall, however, be with you, at all events, in heart. It is certainly fit that the anniversary of this venerable and historical Society, should be celebrated. It is fit that it should publicly recognize the unwelcome fact that its work as yet, is only done in part. It is fit that the surviving representatives and champions of the Anti Slavery cause, should hold this timely and soul-inspiring re-union, and freely confer with each other as to the work of the future, while cherishing the precious memories of the past. And it is fit that they should prepare "an authentic, impartial, and comprehensive record of their action" respecting the grandest battle the world has yet witnessed, for the Rights of Man. This is a duty which they owe alike to themselves and to their country, and its postponement should not be permitted.

Earnestly hoping that your gathering may be largely attended, and that the blessing of God may crown its labors, I am,

Very faithfully yours,

GEO. W. JULIAN.

———

NEWPORT, R. I., April 12, 1875.

WM. STILL, ESQ, *Chairman of Committee, etc.*

Dear Sir:—It would afford me great pleasure to meet the Pennsylvania Society, and to revive the memories of the old times. So rapidly do the years go on, that it is already hard to convince ourselves that slavery has existed during our life-time. It seems, rather, as if its memories were all a dream, or as if we had lived two lives. But the work that it did for our moral development, as individuals, never can be undone; and I hope we are all applying its lessons to the reforms which are still uncompleted.

Very cordially yours, THOS. WENTWORTH HIGGINSON.

73

CHARLESTON, S. C., APRIL 9TH, '75.

To DILLWYN PARRISH and others :—

Dear friends:—I have been honored with your invitation to attend the Centennial Anniversary of "the Pennsylvania Society for promoting the Abolition of Slavery and for the relief of Free Negroes unlawfully held in bondage, and for improving the condition of the African Race," and sincerely regret that it will be impossible to meet with you on that most interesting occasion. The prime purpose for which the Society was organized, as indicated in its title, has been accomplished; its secondary purpose (if it can be considered secondary) the improvement of the condition of the African race, still continues to call for the most earnest and intelligent action of the members of this venerable Society.

Venerable! not so much for its years, as for the character and service of those who founded it, and gave vitality to its beneficent purposes.

Full of sympathy for its past attainments, and with what I believe to be its hopes for the future, I would say as my deliberate judgment, after an experience of nearly thirteen years in the South, and with a full appreciation of all the details to be overcome, that the highest hopes of the Society with reference to the improvement of the colored people are certain of fulfilment.

It is wise to see and understand all the obstacles in the shape of ignorance, vice, and selfishness, that have to be overcome; but it is foolish to be able to see nothing but these.

If the intelligence of the country will do its duty the future is secured. But that is a sham intelligence which seeks to justify its own apathy and indifference by assertions of the hopelessness of attempting to remove the ignorance and vice bequeathed to us by slavery.

The more apparently hopeless the task the more manly and earnestly it should be encountered, and while the members of our old Society in entering upon the second century of its existence may feel that an immense work is yet to be done, they may also feel sure from the past experience of their Society that to brave, and earnest hearts, and wise judgments no work which has for its object the improvement of the condition of man, is impossible of accomplishment.

My faith is unfaltering, notwithstanding the wiles of demagogues, who seek to abuse the confidence of the colored man to his own ruin; the bitterness of that prejudice which seeks to crush him, and the easy facility with which he serves the purposes of both these dangerous foes, that he will yet make a self-respecting and useful citizen. This faith I hold not because-he is a *colored* man, but because he is a *man*.

I am very truly your friend, REUBEN TOMLINSON.

HARRISBURG, PA., April 12th, 1875.

To WILLIAM STILL, ESQ , *of Committee of Arrangements for Anti Slavery Centennial.*

Dear Sir:—Accept my thanks for invitation to be present at your proposed re-union. It would give me great pleasure to accept, but my present engagements and public business forbid. All honor to the noble heroes and heroines of Liberty, who pioneered the path of the True Republic, and to you, who so assiduously encouraged the victim of Oppression on his way to Freedom. God bless the meeting! Yours, very truly,

WILLIAM HOWARD DAY.

MAYOR'S OFFICE, PHILADELPHIA, March 31st, 1875.
W. STILL, ESQR.

Dear Sir:--Your invitation to be present at the "Centennial Anniversary of the Pennsylvania Society, for Promoting the Abolition of Slavery, and for the Relief of Free Negroes Unlawfully held in Bondage, and for Improving the condition of the African Race," to be celebrated on the 14th day of April prox. was received.

I assure you and the gentlemen composing the Committee of Arrangements, that it will afford me much pleasure to be with you on the occasion designated. With respect, I am,

W. S. STOKLEY, *Mayor.*

HAMPTON, VA., April 2, 1875.
MY DEAR MR. STILL :—

Your very kind invitation to the Centennial of the Pennsylvania Abolition Society, is received. I shall be there if I can. The way is hard y clear, for I am compelled to be in Boston at that time, hunting for funds to carry on this school—we are hard pressed—necessity is upon us. Please tell Mr. Parrish that I am too much the slave of my work, to be able to attend, so far as I can now see.

It will be a grand time. The Hampton singers are in the western part of New York State now, and have already made engagements to sing, covering the 14th, and several days later. I am very sorry. We are all of us doing things with all our might. Yours, sincerely,

S. C. ARMSTRONG.

CHICAGO, April 6th, 1875.
DEAR MR. STILL :—

It would be a great pleasure if time and tide would permit, to come to the Centennial of the old Pioneer Society for the Abolition of Slavery. But there is no chance. I must stay home and get my share of your good time through the papers, and send all good wishes to and for those who have the good luck to be present. Very truly yours,

ROBERT COLLYER.

NEW YORK, April 2d, 1875.
Gentlemen :—To attend your celebration would give me the sincerest pleasure. It is precisely one of the things I should rejoice in doing, to live over the glorious days, and to exchange congratulations on the grand achievement. But an anniversary will keep me at home on that very day, the

14th, so that I can only have your thanksgiving through sympathy. I shall, however, share it, sir, that way, and shall remember gratefully, that you invited me to be with you in person as well as in spirit.

Sincerely yours,
O. B. FROTHINGHAM.

EXECUTIVE MANSION, HARRISBURG, Pa.

WILLIAM STILL, ESQ., No. 700 Arch St., Philadelphia, Pa.

Dear Sir:—I shall take great pleasure in attending the Centennial Anniversary of the Pennsylvania Society for Promoting the Abolition of Slavery on Wednesday next, if my health and public engagements here will permit. Respectfully Yours,

J. F. HARTRANFT, Governor.

WESTBURY, 4th Mo. 6, '75.

WILLIAM STILL:

Dear friend:—The kind invitation from the Committee of Arrangements, to unite in celebrating the Centennial Anniversary; it would give us much pleasure to meet the friends and laborers in the cause, and review the past, so full of incident, and so full, too, of blessed and holy memories, which are enshrined on our inner consciousness; but on account of illness in our family circle, fear we shall have to forego the pleasure of being with you. Very respectfully, etc,

JOSEPH & MARY POST.

COLUMBIA, S. C., April 5, 1875.

WILLIAM STILL, ESQ, *Chairman Centennial Anniversary.*

Dear Sir:—I regret that it will be impossible for me to be present at the Centennial meeting, and I wish, through you, to offer my congratulations to those who will be there on the triumph of the cause of universal liberty, which we all had so much at heart, and for which we labored when we scarcely dared hope for success.

The war made many things possible; perhaps as curious as any of the changes, was that my father, Lewis Thompson, should pass the last years of his life in South Carolina, and die peacefully in the State, which, only a few years before, would have hurried him and all his abolition friends to violent death.

I am editing a Republican newspaper here. My brother Lewis, is an army officer, now on leave and visiting me; he also desires to be remembered to the friends in Philadelphia. Very truly, yours,

JAMES G. THOMPSON.

EXECUTIVE MANSION, WASHINGTON, April 6th, 1875.

MR. WILLIAM STILL, 700 *Arch Street, Phila.*

Sir:—The President directs me to acknowledge the receipt of your note, enclosing invitation for the 14th inst., and to convey to you and the members of the Committee, many thanks for the kind attention. He regrets that he will be unable to visit Philadelphia at that time.

I am Sir, very respectfully yours,

LEVI P. LUCKEY, *Secretary.*

PHILADELPHIA, PA., April 1st, 1875.

WILLIAM STILL, ESQ., *Chairman.*

My Dear Sir:—I shall be much pleased to accept the kind invitation with which you have honored me to be present at the Centennial Anniversary of "The Pennsylvania Society for Promoting the Abolition of Slavery and the Relief of Free Negroes Unlawfully held in Bondage, and for improving the Condition of the African Race." The fact of this anniversary occurring on the fourteenth of April, cannot fail to add to the interest of the occasion. Yours, very respectfully,

RUFUS SAXTON.

LINCOLN, LOUDOUN CO., VA., 4th month, 6th, 1875.

To DILLWYN PARRISH, WILLIAM STILL, PASSMORE WILLIAMSON, JOSEPH M. TRUMAN, JR., HENRY M. LANG, Philadelphia.

Respected friends:—I acknowledge the receipt of your kind invitation to attend the Centennial Anniversary of the Pennsylvania Society, for Promoting the Abolition of Slavery. It would give me much pleasure to participate in the meetings proposed to be held, but I have no prospect of being present, and must content myself with the expression of my sincere desire that your proceedings may tend to elucidate and preserve, for the benefit of posterity, many important facts in the history of the Anti-Slavery cause.

That great system of wrong, American Slavery, has come to an end; not in the way that we anticipated, but in the ordering of Divine Providence, by means that could not be foreseen by human wisdom, nor frustrated by human depravity.

There remains yet a great work to be done, in promoting the moral elevation and religious instruction of the colored race in this country. On the success of this work depends not only their welfare, but the prosperity of the American Union, which can only be sustained by the virtue and intelligence of the people. Very Respectfully your friend,

SAML. M. JANNEY.

MEMORANDUM OF ANTI-SLAVERY ACTION IN THE DISTRICT OF COLUMBIA AND VIRGINIA.

BY SAMUEL M. JANNEY.

As one of the purposes intended by the Pennsylvania Abolition Society, in celebrating their Centennial Anniversary, is "to present an impartial and comprehensive record of their action, as well as a general history of the Anti-Slavery cause," I deem it proper to give some account of efforts made to promote that cause in the District of Columbia and the northern part of Virginia.

About fifty years ago, there existed in Washington city an Anti-Slavery Society, the title of which I do not remember, and in Alexandria, then a part of the District of Columbia, we had an association composed mostly of Friends, and a few Methodists, called the Benevolent Society of Alexandria, for ameliorating and improving the condition of the people of color. To rescue from the possession of slave traders persons illegally held in bondage, and to enlighten the public mind in regard to the evils of slavery, were two of the main objects we had in view.

I think these Societies were, at one time, represented in a convention held in Philadelphia, by invitation of the Pennsylvania Abolition Society.

At that time the domestic slave trade was actively carried on in Washington and Alexandria, and among its victims were some who were free-born, or were slaves only for a term of years. These we sometimes succeeded in rescuing by a legal process, but not unfrequently, they were carried off by the traders before we received information of their captivity. On behalf of the Benevolent Society a series of essays were written on slavery and the domestic slave trade, which, in the year 1827, were published in the Alexandria Gazette, a paper that had a considerable circulation in Virginia. The opposition to such publications was not then so great in Virginia, as it became a few years later, and the views we promulgated, adverse to Slavery, were read without producing any demonstrations of violence. Slavery was then generally acknowledged to be an evil entailed upon us by former generations, which, it was alleged, could not be removed without much danger: and most of the slaveholders maintained that the slaves, when liberated, must be colonized in some foreign country.

The Benevolent Society of Alexandria in conjunction with the Anti-Slavery Society in Washington, about the year 1827, got up a petition to Congress for the abolition of slavery, and the slave trade in the District of Columbia. We obtained the signatures of about a thousand respectable citizens, among whom were prominent merchants and judges of the District Courts. I remember that while soliciting signatures, I called on George Washington Park Custis, the proprietor of the Arlington estate. He treated me with civility, and admitted the evils of slavery, but declined to sign the petition. He spoke freely of the unproductiveness of slave labor, and said, " I am accounted the third among the richest men of Virginia, and yet I seldom have a dollar." His patriotism shone forth in his eloquent orations, but he made no efforts, nor submitted to any sacrifices to remove an evil that, I believe, he sincerely deplored. He did, however, follow the example of Washington, by providing in his will for the liberation of his slaves.

Our petition was presented to Congress, and although it seemed to produce no immediate effect, it was in subsequent years, sometimes referred to, in the earnest debates that took place on the subject of Slavery. We did not petition for the *immediate* abolition of Slavery, which would have been a just and safe measure, but in deference to the prejudices of many whose signatures were solicited, we asked that a law of Congress might be passed, declaring that all children of slaves born in the District, after the 4th of July, 1828, should be free at the age of 25 years, and that laws might be enacted to prevent slaves being removed from the District, or brought in for sale, hire or transportation. If this measure, inadequate as it appears, had been adopted, it might have led to similar legislation in Maryland and Virginia, and possibly the awful calamity of civil war might have been averted.

I have no records to show any further action of the Anti-Slavery Associations in Washington and Alexandria. After some years they ceased to exist, but some of those who had been members of them, continued to feel the same interest in the cause of human liberty, and to manifest their zeal by publications showing the disastrous effects of Slavery.

In the years 1844 and 1845, a number of essays over the signature of a Virginian were published,—showing the injustice and impolicy of Slaveholding, and pointing out the benefits that would result from emancipation. Some of these essays were published in the Saturday Visitor of Baltimore, edited by Dr. J. E. Snodgrass; some in the Alexandria Gazette, and others in the Richmond Whig, an influential paper edited by J. Hampden Pleasants. Extra numbers of the papers were purchased for distribution, and several of the essays were printed in pamphlet form, and extensively circulated in Maryland and Virginia.

The funds to pay for printing were mostly contributed by Friends in Philadelphia.

———

AMESBURY, 11th, 4 Mo., 1875.

To DILLWYN PARISH :

Dear Friend: The enclosed document has been forwarded to me by an eminent lawyer of Richmond, Va. (also enclosed) requesting me to present it to the Centennial meeting. It speaks for itself. Nothing more severely condemnatory of slavery was ever spoken by Garrison or Sumner, or acted by John Brown, than this noble and Christian testimony of Richard Randolph, the brother of John Randolph, of Roanoke.

Does it not forcibly recall that wonderful death-scene so graphically depicted by thy father who was called to witness the bequest of liberty to his slaves by John Randolph? Surely there was something noble and generous in the blood of those old Virginians!

If the Pennsylvania Abolition Society need any justification of its doings for a century past it is furnished by this document. For its object has been to save men from the condition so sternly characterized by the testator as barbarous and cruel, and infamous; a lawless and monstrous tyranny.

Let us thank the Divine Providence that we have been permitted to see the end of the "accursed thing," against which Richard Randolph bore his emphatic testimony. I am truly thy friend,

JOHN G. WHITTIER.

RICHARD RANDOLPH'S WILL.

To all whom it may Concern : I, Richard Randolph, jun'r of Bozarre, in
the County of Cumberland, of sound mind and memory, do make this
writing—written with my own hand and subscribed with my name, this
eighteenth day of February in the twentieth year of the American independence, to be my last will and testament, in form and substance as follows :

In the first place, to make retribution, as far as I am able, to an
unfortunate race of bondmen, over whom my ancestors have usurped and
exercised the most lawless and monstrous tyranny, and in whom my
countrymen by their iniquitous laws, in contradiction of their own declaration of rights, and in violation of every sound law of nature, of the inherent,
inalienable and imprescriptible rights of man ; and of every moral and
political honesty, have vested me with absolute property. To express my
abhorrence of the theory as well as infamous practice of usurping the
rights of our fellow-creatures equally entitled with ourselves to the enjoyment of liberty and happiness. To exculpate myself to those who may
perchance to think or hear of me after death from the black crime, which
might otherwise be imputed to me, of voluntarily holding the above-
mentioned miserable beings in the same state of abject slavery in which I
found them on receiving my patrimony at lawful age. To impress my
children with just horror at a crime so enormous and indelible. To conjure them in the last words of a fond father never to participate in it in
any—the remotest degree, however sanctioned by laws (framed by the
tyrants themselves who oppress them), or supported by false reasoning
used always to veil the sordid views of avarice and the lust of power. To
declare to them and to the world that nothing but uncontrollable necessity
—forced on me by my father, who wrongfully bound over men to satisfy
the rapacious creditors of a brother—who for this purpose, which he falsely
believed to be generous, mortgaged all his slaves to British harpies, for
money to gratify pride and pamper sensuality ; by which mortgage the
said slaves being bound, I could not exercise the right of ownership necessary to their emancipation ; and being obliged to keep them on my land
was driven reluctantly to violate them in a great degree (though I trust
far less than others have done) in order to maintain them ; that nothing,
I say, short of this necessity should have forced me to an act which my
soul abhors. For the aforesaid purposes, and with an indignation too
great for utterance at the tyrants of the earth—from the throned despot
of a whole nation to the most despicable but not less infamous petty tor-
mentor of a single wretched slave, whose torture constitutes his wealth and
enjoyment. I do *truly* declare that it is my will and desire, nay, most
anxious wish, that my negroes, all of them, be liberated, and I do declare
them, by this writing, free and emancipated to all intents and purposes
whatsoever : fully and freely exonerated from all further service to my
heirs, executors or assigns, and altogether as free as the illiberal laws will
permit them to be. I mean herein to include all and every slave of which
I die possessed or to which I have any claim by inheritance or otherwise.
I thus yield them up their liberty basely wrested from them by my fore-

fathers and beg, humbly beg, their forgiveness for the manifold injuries I have too often inhumanly, unjustly and mercilessly inflicted on them. And I do further declare that it is my will, that if I shall be so unfortunate as to die possessed of any slaves (which I will not do if I can ever be enabled to emancipate them legally) and the 'said slaves shall be liable for my father's debts and sold for them; that in that case five hundred pounds be raised from my other estate, real or personal, as my wife shall think best, and in any manner she may choose and applied to the purchase at such sale of such of the said miserable slaves as have been most worthy; to be judged of by my said wife, which said slaves I do hereby declare free as soon as they are purchased to all intents and purposes whatsoever; and in case I emancipate the said slaves (which I shall surely do the first moment possible) I do devise, give and bequeath to them the said slaves, four hundred acres of my land, to be laid off as my wife shall direct, and to be given to the heads of families in proportion to the number of the children and the merits of the parties, as my said wife shall judge for the best. The land to be laid off where and how my said wife shall direct, and to be held by the said slaves when allotted to them in fee. I do likewise conjure my said wife to lend every assistance to the said slaves thro' life in her power; and to rear our children up to the same practice and leave it on them as her latest injunction—and to do everything directed above relative to the said slaves.

I now proceed to direct the manner in which my other property is to be disposed of (having fulfilled this first and greatest duty and most anxious and zealous wish to befriend the miserable and persecuted of whatsoever nation, color or degree), by my will as here seen written on this and another sheet of paper, each signed by my own hand and with my own name and connected together by wafers.

R'D RANDOLPH, JUN'R.

In the second place, I give and bequeath to my wife, Judith Randolph all my personal estate remaining of whatsoever nature animate, inanimate in possession or in action, claimed or to be claimed, right or title whatsoever to her sole use and disposal forever that [torn out] exclusive of slaves. I likewise give, devise and bequeath to my said wife all my real estate whatsoever of which I die possessed and also all to which I have any claim or title whatsoever to her and to her heirs, in full confidence that she will do the most ample justice to our children by making them independent as soon as they are of age—if she remains single—or by securing them a comfortable support by settlement on them before any marriage into which she may hereafter resolve to enter (which if she do marry will be the only certain mode of providing for them) and by educating them as well as her fortune will enable her. The only anxiety I feel on their account arises from a fear of her maternal tenderness leading her to too great indulgence of them, against which I beg leave thus to caution her. I now consign them to her affectionate love, desiring that they be educated in some profession—or trade if they be incapable of a liberal profession, and that they be instructed in virtue and in the most zealous principles of liberty and manly independence. I dedicate them to that virtue and that liberty which I trust will protect their infancy and of which I conjure them to be the indefatigable and incorruptible supporters through life. I request my wife frequently to read this my will to my tenderly beloved children, that they may know something of their father's heart when they have forgotten his person. Let them be virtuous and free —the rest is vain.

Finally, I entreat my wife to consider the above confidence as the strongest possible proof of the estimation and ardent love which I have always uniformly felt for her and which must be the latest impulse of my heart.

I hereby appoint my said wife sole executrix of this my last will and testament, but in case I should be so unfortunate as to be left by her single and die without any other will than this executed by me, I appoint in that case as my executors (requesting their attention to my injunction on my wife above mentioned, relying on them to execute them and the directions in my said will as she will otherwise do) to-wit, the following most esteemed friends: my father-in-law, S. George Tucker, my brother, John Randolph, my friends, Ryland Randolph. Brett Randolph, Creed Taylor, John Thompson, Alexander Campbell, Daniel Call, and the most virtuous and incorruptible of mankind and next to my father-in-law—my greatest benefactor, George Wythe, Chancellor of Virginia—the brightest ornament of human nature. I rely on the aforementioned virtuous friends for the punctual execution of my will, the care and guardianship of my children, in case of the death of my wife either before or after me (to whom if she live I have entrusted them solely); and to those of them most nearly connected with me by friendship I look for assistance of my family after my death in all cases of difficulty. If any among them do not choose to undertake the task imposed on them by me, I beg them not to do so from motives of generosity or delicacy; and to excuse the liberty which (it may appear to some of them least intimately acquainted with me) I have taken in thus calling on them.

In witness of the above directions, which I again declare to be my will and testament, drawn by me from calm reflections, I have hereunto subscribed my name and affixed my seal the day and year aforesaid.

R'd RANDOLPH, JUN'R., [seal]

Signed and sealed in the presence
of the following persons and
declared to be the last will of
the above named Richard Randolph, junr.

RYLAND RANDOLPH.

At a District Court, held at Prince Edward Court-house, April 8th, 1797.

This last will and testament of Richard Randolph jun'r, deceased, was presented in court by Judith Randolph, executrix therein named, there being but one witness to said will, and he not being in court, Miller Woodson and Peter Johnson being sworn, severally deposed that they are well acquainted with the testator's handwriting, and verily believe that the said will and the name thereto subscribed are all of the testator's proper handwriting. Whereupon the said will is ordered to be recorded. And on motion of the executrix, therein named, who gave bond with John Randolph, Brett Randolph, and Creed Taylor, her securities, in the penalty of twelve thousand pounds and took the oath required by law, certificate for obtaining a probate thereof in due form is granted her.

Teste,

F. WATKINS, C. D. C.

A Copy—Teste

B. J. WORSHAM,
C'lk Prince Edward Circ. Sup'r Court.

———

Enon Valley, Pa., 8 April, 1875.

To Wm. Still, Esq., *Chairman:*—

I have received your invitation to be present at the Centennial Anniversary of "The Pennsylvania Society for promoting [the abolition of slavery; and for the relief of Free Negroes, &c."

As time is making such fast inroads upon the ranks of the Abolitionists it would indeed be pleasant to look once more into each other's faces before we die. I have an errand to Philadelphia some time the coming Summer, and have been trying, since the receipt of your letter, to arrange matters so they would allow me to attend the contemplated meeting. But it is impossible to do so, and instead of going in person, I must send this letter of excuse.

It gives me great pleasure to learn, what indeed I might have suspected, that the Society, now that slavery is passed away, devote their funds to sustaining *schools of instruction* among the Freedmen. I regard education as the sovereign panacea for all the troubles of the South; and for the colored man his only salvation, As in Natural History we find that the grey and black squirrels disappear in our forests when the red squirrel predominates; and as the brown rat takes his departure when the Norway rat makes his appearance; so, the other races of mankind yield to the superior power and sagacity of the Anglo Saxon.

There is but one exception to this rule. The *Negro* holds his own with our proud race, and can live and thrive with us—*provided* he is *educated.* The next census will show, I apprehend, that under all the trials of the transition state from slavery to freedom he has not retrograded in any respect, but has positively improved in soul, body, and estate.

I have had from childhood a warm attachment to the colored people; and were I possessed of millions I would be glad to appropriate them to the establishment of the best schools and libraries among them every where, believing that education and refinement, by making them *really* equal with the whites, would supercede the necessity for Civil Rights Bills, and do more for them than anything else.

Hoping you will have a good time at the reunion, and regretting sincerely that I cannot be there, I remain, with much respect, yours,

A. B. Bradford.

www.ingramcontent.com/pod-product-compliance
Lightning Source LLC
Chambersburg PA
CBHW021424090426
42742CB00009B/1248